Studies in the History of Art VOLUME 9

NATIONAL GALLERY OF ART, WASHINGTON

This publication was produced by the Editor's Office, National Gallery of Art, Washington.
Printed by Eastern Press, New Haven, Connecticut.
The type is Sabon, set by Composition Systems Incorporated, Arlington, Virginia.
The text paper is Warren's Patina and the cover is Mead Moistrite matte.
Designed by Susan Lehmann, Washington.

Cover: Giovanni Bellini, *Portrait of a Condottiere (Portrait of Giovanni Emo).* National Gallery of Art, Washington, Samuel H. Kress Collection

Contents

A Portrait of Giovanni Emo in the National Gallery of Art

ANNE MARKHAM SCHULZ

In spite of several attempts to name the sitter in the so-called *Portrait of a Condottiere* attributed to Giovanni Bellini in the National Gallery of Art in Washington (figs. 1, 2), his identity has so far eluded discovery.[1] Gronau and Tietze identified the portrait with Giovanni Bellini's "ritratto picolo de M. Jacomo Marcello" listed by Marc'Antonio Michiel.[2] Suida recognized in the painting Bellini's portrait of Bartolomeo d'Alviano recorded by Vasari.[3] Bertelè, among others, called the sitter Bartolomeo Colleoni; Heinemann proposed Vittore Pavoni.[4] Authenticated images of these four persons preserved in statues, medals, and paintings explain the lack of unanimity among critics: the sitter in Bellini's portrait resembles none of the persons supposed to be Bellini's *Condottiere.*

He does, however, look so much like Giovanni Emo, as Emo appears in his effigy attributed to Antonio Rizzo (figs. 3, 4, 5), that it would seem unnecessary to belabor the point with detailed analyses.[5] Indeed, what differences exist are due, not to differences of physiognomy, but to differences of medium and style. Whereas, the sculptured portrait reflects the influence of the exaggerated features and leonine expression of Verrocchio's *Colleoni*, the painted portrait betrays the generalizing stereometry of heads by Antonello da Messina superimposed upon the graphic definition of individual features derived from Mantegna.

A detail difficult to see in the painting—the locks of hair which emerge from beneath the cap and are gathered at the nape—serves to reinforce the likeness. Both figures wear the same soft high cap tilted very slightly downward on the right and a high-collared cloak fastened on the right shoulder. A mid-eighteenth-century watercolor drawing of the statue by Johannes Grevembroch (fig. 6) indicates that the limestone figure was formerly polychromed and that the

[1] The painting (no. 335) on wood, measures 0.49 x 0.35 cm (19¼ x 13⅞ in.); Samuel H. Kress Collection, 1939, no. 335. See Fern Rusk Shapley, *Paintings from the Samuel H. Kress Collection. Italian Schools, XV-XVI Century* (London, 1968), 40f., no. K413.

[2] Georg Gronau, *Giovanni Bellini, des Meisters Gemälde* (Stuttgart/Berlin, 1930), 205, n. 72; Hans Tietze, "At the National Gallery of Art: Giovanni Bellini's *Portrait of Giacomo Marcello,*" *Gazette des Beaux-Arts, 89* (May-June 1947): 148f. For the listing by Michiel, See *Der Anonimo Morelliano,* ed. Theodor Frimmel (Vienna, 1896), 90.

[3] William E. Suida, "Giovanni Bellini's Portrait of the Condottiere Bartolomeo d'Alviano," *Art Quarterly, 13* (1950): 48ff.; and Giorgio Vasari, *Le vite de' più eccellenti pittori scultori ed architettori,* ed. Gaetano Milanesi (Florence, 1878), *3*: 170.

[4] Tommaso Bertelè, "Iconografia di Bartolomeo Colleoni," *Bergomum, 24* (1950): 13ff; and Fritz Heinemann, *Giovanni Bellini e i Belliniani* (Venice, 1962), *1*: 224, V.46.As long ago as 1786 the painting was believed to represent Bartolomeo Colleoni.

[5] The *Effigy of Emo* is currently exhibited in the courtyard of the Museo Civico at Vicenza; see Franco Barbieri, *Il Museo Civico di Vicenza. Dipinti e sculture dal xiv al xv secolo* (Venice, 1962), 229ff. I am most grateful to Professors Martin Kubelick and Lynda Fairbairn for photographing the figure for me.

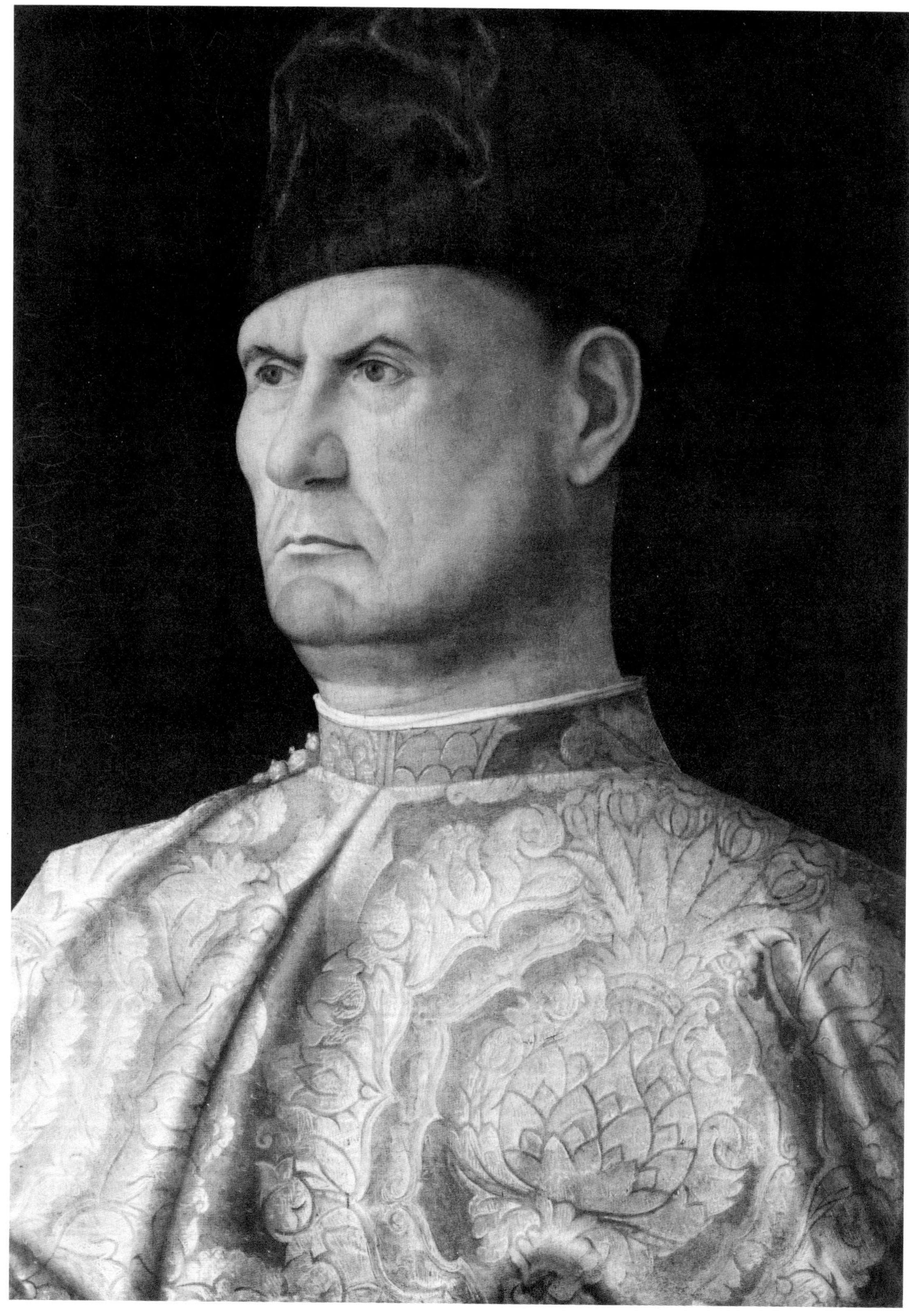

Fig. 1. Giovanni Bellini, Portrait of a Condottiere (Portrait of Giovanni Emo), *c. 1475-1483. Wood. National Gallery of Art, Washington, Samuel H. Kress Collection.*

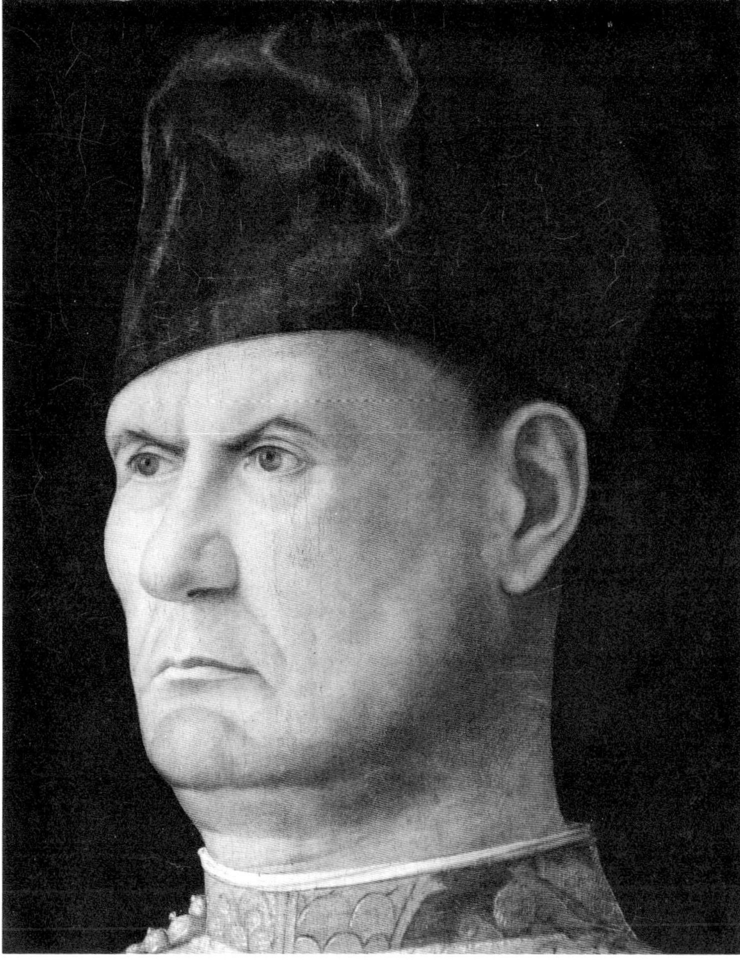

Fig. 2. Giovanni Bellini, Portrait of a Condottiere *(detail of fig. 1)*

polychromy of Emo's cloak and robe simulated brocade.[6] Grevembroch used black for the hat and yellow and gold for the brocade; in the painting the figure's hat is royal blue, while the cloak is crimson and gold brocade.

Giovanni di Giorgio Emo was born in 1425. As Venetian senator he participated in the elections of Doges Tron, Marcello, and Vendramin. On three significant occasions he occupied the high office of ambassador. In 1474 Emo was sent to Matthias Corvinus of Hungary to persuade him to ally himself with Venice in the war against the Turks. In the following year Emo met with Sultan Mahommet II at Constantinople. In 1478 he was chosen to speak for Venice during the crisis which followed the Pazzi conspiracy at Florence. He served at Brescia as Venetian *Capitanio* and oversaw the reenforcement of Udine against the invasion of the Turks. Upon the death of Antonio Loredan in 1482, Emo was made *Provveditore Generale* in the war against Ferrara. As the highest-ranking Venetian civilian in that military campaign, he advised the commander of the troops and reported on the commander's actions to the senate. Under Emo, the conquest of the Polesine was rapidly concluded with the taking of Lendinara and Badia. At the battle of Stellata in September 1483

[6]Venice, Museo Civico Correr, MS. Gradenigo-Dolfin 49, Johannes Grevembroch, *Gli abiti de Veneziani di quasi ogni età con diligenza raccolti e dipinti nel secolo xviii,* 1:38.

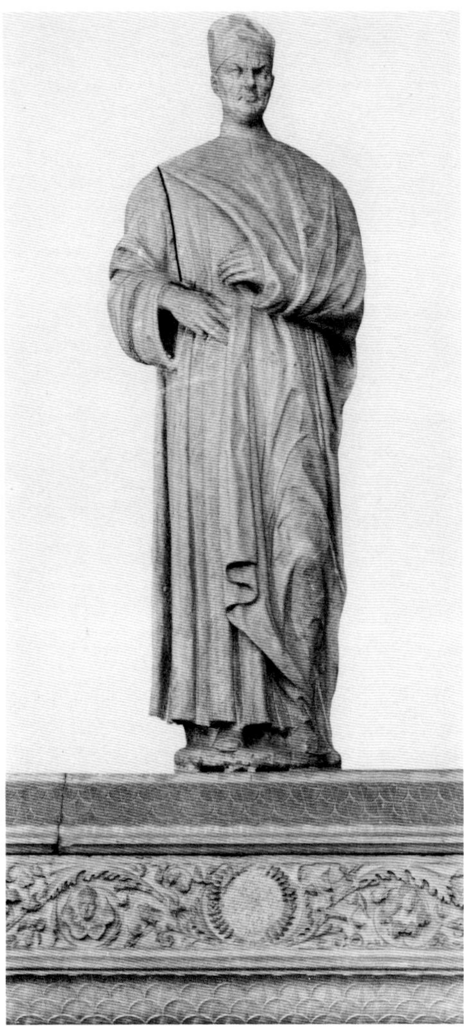

Fig. 3. Attributed to Antonio Rizzo, Effigy of Giovanni Emo, *c. 1485. Stone. Museo Civico, Vicenza*

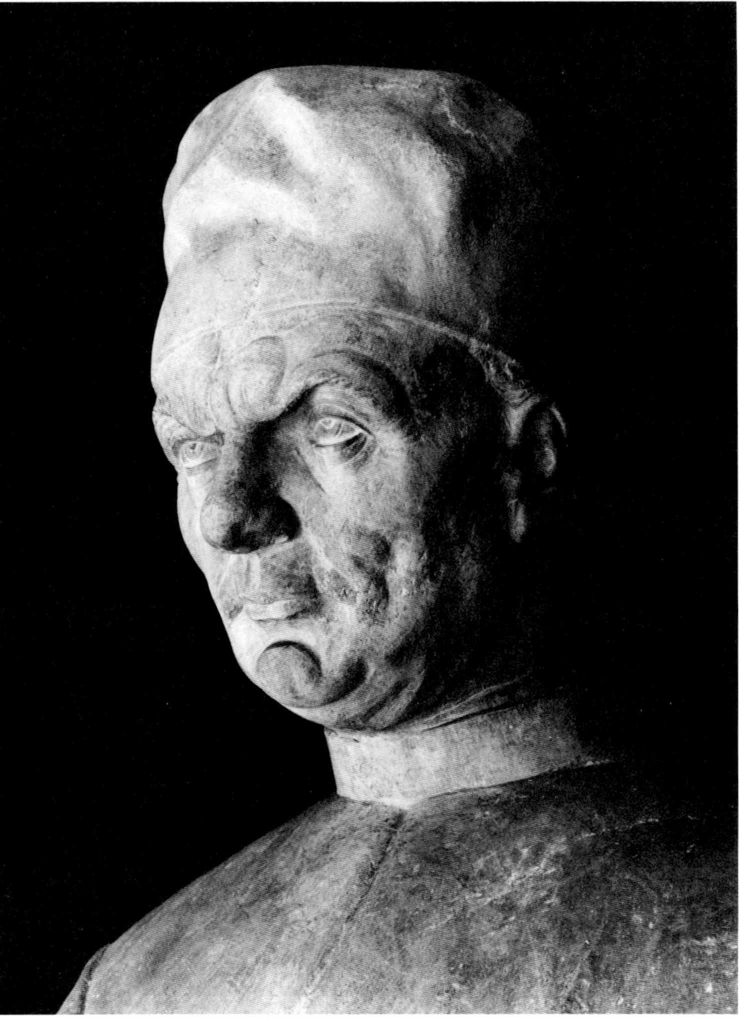

Fig. 4. Attributed to Antonio Rizzo, Effigy of Giovanni Emo *(detail of fig. 3)*

Emo was hurt by his falling horse. He died on September 15, 1483, and was buried in a tomb erected by his sons in Santa Maria dei Servi, Venice.[7]

The costume which Emo wears undoubtedly served to identify his office; unfortunately it is no longer possible to say with certainty what that office was. The most detailed description of the costumes of Venetian officials is that published by Cesare Vecellio in 1590. The habits of both ambassadors and "Generali di Venetia in tempo di guerra" described by Vecellio possess features common to the habit of the effigy and portrait of Emo, but neither corresponds entirely.[8] According to Vecellio, both ambassadors and generals wore cloaks fastened with gold buttons on one shoulder: ambassadors' cloaks were fastened on the left; generals' cloaks were fastened on the right. Cloaks of generals were explicitly described as golden.[9] Both the fastening and color of Emo's cloak speak in favor of the habit of a general, as does the absence of a gold necklace customarily worn by ambassadors. But Emo is portrayed wearing a hat which is very

[7] For the biography of Giovanni Emo, see Sebastiano Rumor, *Storia breve degli Emo* (Vicenza, n.d.), 63-68; and Venice, Museo Civico Correr, MS. Cicogna 1536, Giuseppe Giacinto Bergantini, "Memorie della famiglia Emo P. V. esistenti nel monastero de' Servi di Venezia," in *Memorie spettanti alla città e dominio di Venezia,* 290-303. The date of Emo's death was discovered by Flaminio Corner, *Ecclesiae Venetae antiquis monumentis* (Venice, 1749), 2:53, in a diary of the convent of the Venetian Servi.

[8] Cesare Vecellio, *De gli habiti antichi, et moderni di diverse parti del mondo libri due* (Venice, 1590), pp. 84 rf., 102 rf. Seventeenth-, eighteenth-, and nineteenth-century Venetian costume books consistently rely on Vecellio for earlier costumes.

[9] Further evidence of the adoption of the golden

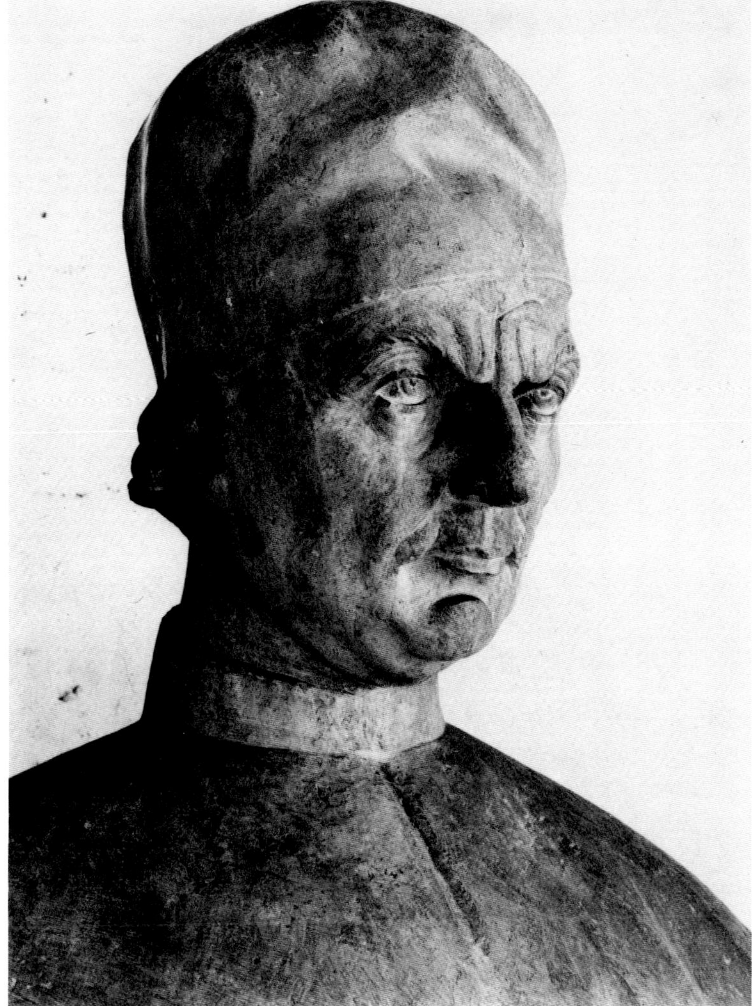

Fig. 5. Attributed to Antonio Rizzo, Effigy of Giovanni Emo *(detail of fig. 3)*

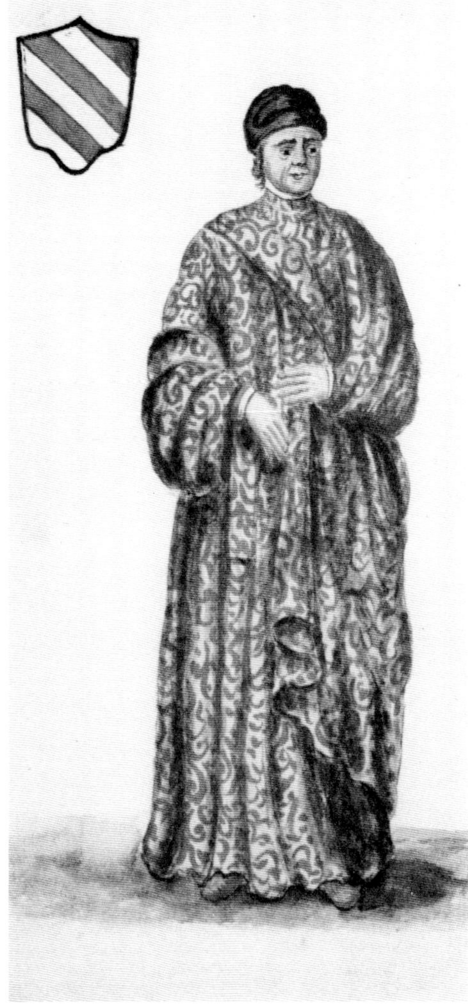

Fig. 6. Johannes Grevembroch, Watercolor illustration for Gli abiti de Veneziani di quasi ogni etè . . . *(c. mid-18th century), 1:*38 (MS. Gradenigo-Dolfin 49). Museo Civico Correr, Venice.

similar to the *berretta* assigned by Vecellio to ambassadors—not the hat of a Venetian general.[10] It may be that the dress of various officials underwent minor modifications in the course of a century. Or perhaps Vecellio's rubric, "Generale," referred only to military commanders, while civilian *Provveditori Generali* wore a slightly different costume.

Identification of the sitter in Bellini's so-called *Portrait of a Condottiere* with Giovanni Emo permits the postulation, for its date of execution, of a *terminus ante quem* of 1483, the date of Emo's death. In 1483 Emo was fifty-eight years old. The subject of Bellini's portrait can hardly be supposed to be a great deal younger. Thus we gain an approximate date of c. 1475-1483 for Bellini's portrait as well.

cloak by military leaders comes from Vincenzo Coronelli, *Isolario dell'atlante veneto* (Venice, 1696), *1*:45, according to whom the *Capitano del Mar,* Orsato Giustiniani (d. 1464) bequeathed to the church of San Andrea della Certosa "anche il suo Manto Generalitio di soprariccio d'oro."

[10] Generals' hats had flat tops broader than their bases, as can be seen in the *Effigy of General Benedetto Pesaro* (d. 1503) from his tomb in Santa Maria dei Frari, Venice.

Dürer's *Melencolia I*: The Limits of Knowledge

PHILIP L. SOHM

From the scant written evidence surviving from the early sixteenth-century about Dürer's *Melencolia I* (fig. 1), it is known that the artist distributed this renowned engraving together with *St. Jerome in his Study* (fig. 2) and that the learned discussed one engraving in association with the other.[1] Whether Dürer designed the two engravings dated 1514 as pendants remains moot, but their later association in the artist's and public's minds should be recognized as more significant than coincidental. When they are considered together, the *Melencolia I* and *St. Jerome* contrast the transcendent tranquility of sacred learning with the joyless frustrations of secular knowledge.[2] The spiritual comforts of St. Jerome's theological pursuits are vividly expressed by his ordered, luminous study and serve as a poignant foil to the frustrations of Melancholy's rationalistic cogitations, embodied by the disarray of objects scattered around her damp, crepuscular abode. In Panofsky's estimation, this contrast is "too perfect to be accidental. While St. Jerome is comfortably installed at his writing desk, the winged Melancholia sits in a crouching position . . . on a low slab of stone by an unfinished building."[3] An antithesis of sacred and secular learning was indeed foremost in Dürer's mind but not necessarily in the sense surmised by Panofsky. Rather, it can be established that Dürer intended to juxtapose the two polarities of intellectual endeavor within the single image of *Melencolia I*.

Whereas the iconography of *St. Jerome* is readily accessible, the unprecedented complexity of *Melencolia I* has generated a comparable morass of interpretations. It has been analyzed alchemically, astrologically, and psychoanalytically;[4] it has been understood as an illustration of saturnine, Neoplatonic melancholy, as a tribute to the scientist Johann Müller, as a Christian paradox, and as an exhorta-

[1] On his trip to the Netherlands in 1520, Dürer distributed the two engravings to at least eight individuals: Hans Rupprich, ed., *Dürer: Schriftlicher Nachlass* (Berlin, 1956), *1:* 156. In 1515, Anton Tucher sold three pair(*1:* 295). See also the letter from Johann Cochlaeus to Pirckheimer, Apr. 5, 1520 (*1:* 265). *Melencolia I* measures 24.0 x 18.7 cm (9⁷⁄₁₆ x 7³⁄₈ in); R. Horace Gallatin Collection, National Gallery of Art, B-15,223.

[2] For a most eloquent description of Melancholy's depression, see H. Wölfflin, "Zur Interpretation von Dürers Melancholie," *Jahrbuch für Kunstwissenschaft, 1* (1923): 175-181. The bibliography on the engraving is too extensive to list here, much less to review; all contributions prior to 1971 are included in M. Mende, *Dürer-Bibliographie* (Wiesbaden, 1971), 246-251, with the exception of a lengthy, but unconvincing, alchemical interpretation by Calvesi ("A noir. Melencolia I," *Storia dell'Arte, 1* [1969]: 37-96). For literature appearing during the Dürer year of 1971, see W. Stechow, "Recent Dürer Studies," *Art Bulletin, 56* (1974): 259-270. The most important article published recently is by K. Hoffman, "Dürers 'Melencolia'," *Kunst als Bedeutungsträger. Gedenkschrift für Günter Bandmann,* ed. W. Busch, R. Haussherr and E. Trier (Berlin, 1978), 251-277.

[3] Erwin Panofsky, *The Life and Art of Albrecht Dürer* (Princeton, 1943), *1:* 156.

[4] G. F. Hartlaub, "Arcana Artis," *Zeitschrift für Kunstgeschichte,* 6 (1937): 302-314; J. Read, "Dürer's Melencolia: an alchemical interpretation," *Burlington Magazine, 87* (1945): 283-284; Calvesi, "A noir," 37-96. A. Warburg, "Heidnisch-Antike Weissagung in Wort und Bild zu Luthers Zeiten" in *Gesammelte Schriften* (Leipzig-Berlin, 1932), 526-

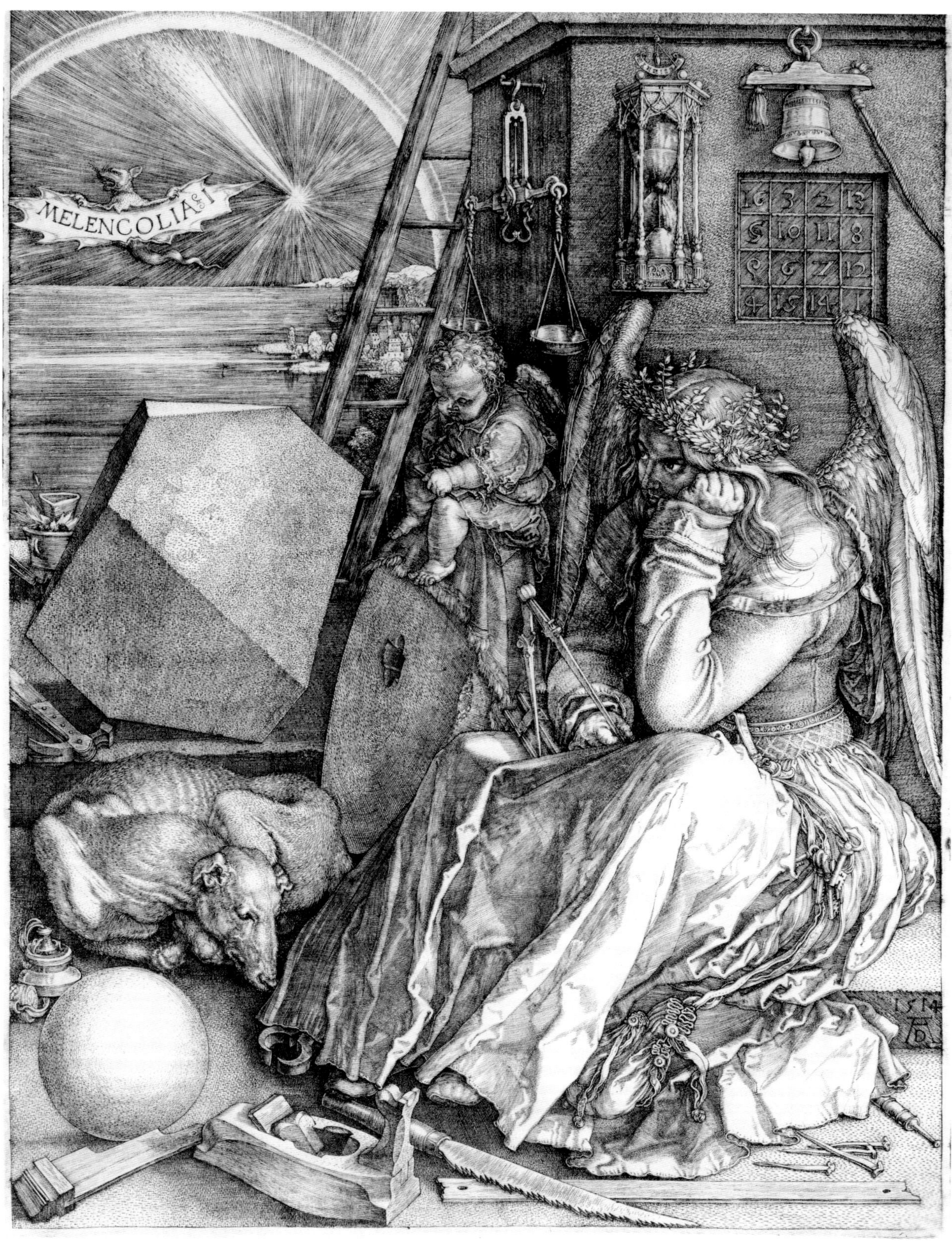

Fig. 1. Albrecht Dürer, Melencolia I, *1514. Engraving. National Gallery of Art, Washington, R. Horace Gallatin Collection*

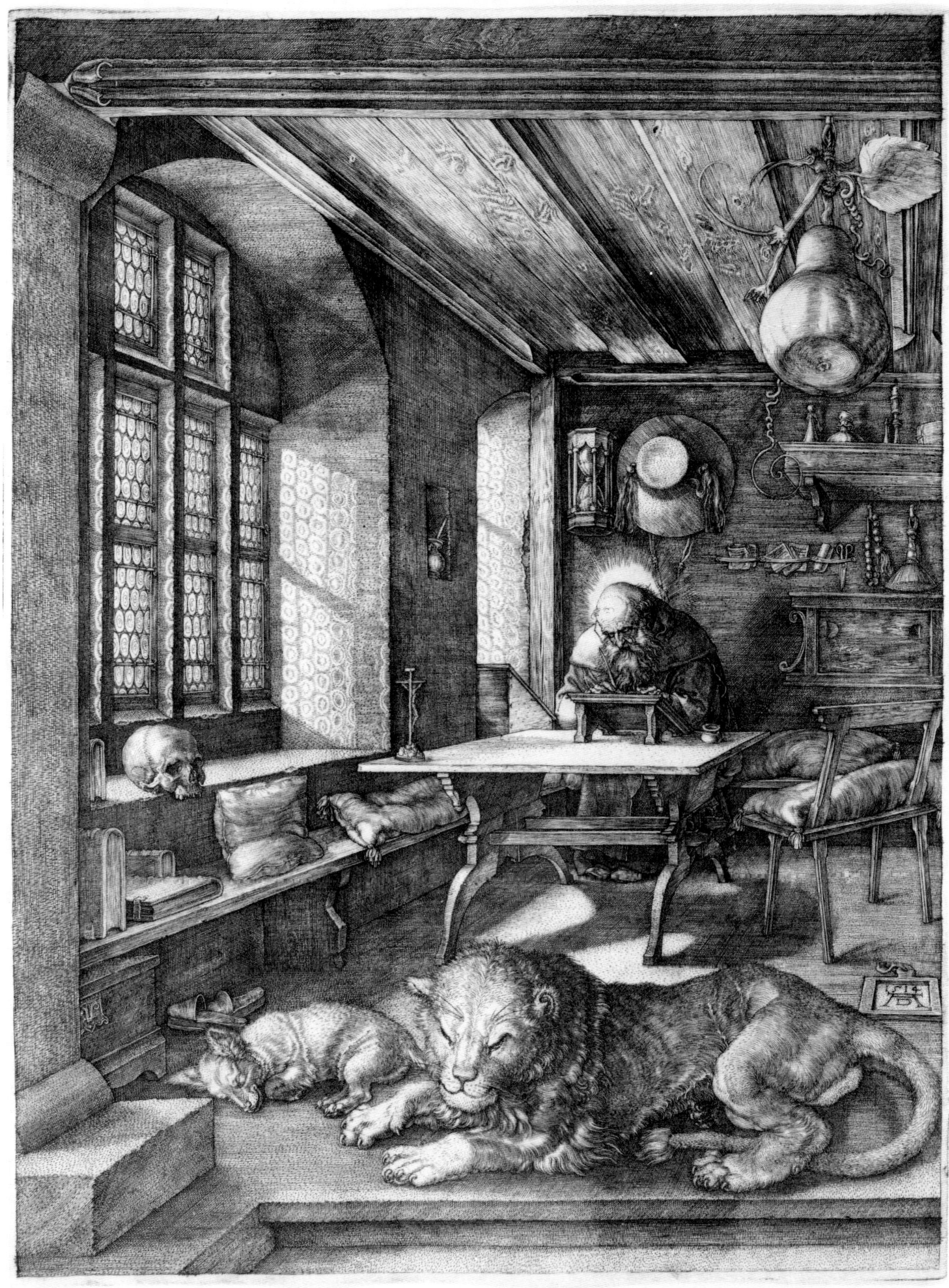

Fig. 2. Albrecht Dürer, St. Jerome in his Study, *1514. Engraving, National Gallery of Art, Washington, R. Horace Gallatin Collection*

tion against the fear of a second flood, to mention only a few of the many theories.[5]

Undoubtedly the most widely accepted and most plausible interpretation is that of Panofsky, who concluded that Dürer incorporated, through the medium of Saturn, the imagery of geometry—the governing principle of art—with the Neoplatonic conception of melancholy as divine inspiration and thereby created a geometer's or artist's Melancholy.[6] Under the influence of Saturn, the potent star of all melancholics, the melancholic imagination could be led to remarkable achievements in the arts. The tools and instruments represent the Saturnine abilities of the melancholic in pure geometry and its applications in art and architecture. The dog, subject to depression and madness, and the bat, because of its nocturnal habits, refer to the melancholic temperament. The magic square on the wall and the wreath of lovage worn by Melancholy are talismans used to attract the healing influence of Jupiter to offset the excess of Saturn. "The keys mean power, the purse means wealth," wrote Dürer, probably referring to his belief that power (or mastery) and wealth are the rewards of the artist who uses geometry.

To assimilate the diverse ideas of Saturn, geometry, and melancholy, Dürer, Panofsky argues, turned to the German philosopher Cornelius Agrippa von Nettesheim and specifically to his *De Occulta Philosophia,* which Panofsky assumes Dürer knew in manuscript form prior to its publication in 1531. Based on Marsilio Ficino's transformation of melancholy from its medieval definition as despondent acedia into a Neoplatonic afflatus, Agrippa envisioned three types of melancholy, each associated with man's three faculties of perception. *Melancholia imaginativa,* inspired by Saturn, is cognitively limited to the physical world and hence inspires the practitioners of geometry such as astronomers, architects, and artists. Panofsky concludes that *melancholia imaginativa,* as the lowest of the three mental faculties, was identified by Dürer with the roman numeral I.[7]

Yet one feels an uneasy ambivalence about the inspirational power attributed by Agrippa and Panofsky to Dürer's image of a sullen, passive Melancholy. Agrippa characterized the melancholic state as a "frenzy": "this *humor melancholicus* has such power that they say it attracts certain daemons into our bodies, through whose presence and activity men fall into ecstasies and pronounce many wonderful things"; and, as a result, they become "so outstanding by their genius that they seemed gods rather than men."[8] If the melancholic mind, as defined by Agrippa, is elevated above all other mortal thought and approaches the divine when it is inspired by *furor divinus,* surely Dürer's Melancholy, despite her attributes, does not seem psychologically akin to Agrippa's melancholic genius. The apparent variance of Agrippa's description of melancholy with Dürer's image does not mean that Agrippa could not have been Dürer's source, as some scholars have suggested.[9] Rather, it can be established through new evidence that Dürer's Melancholy had indeed experienced a condition similar to Agrippa's melancholic afflatus. If the engraving is read as a temporal sequence, as Dürer intended, with an implied past and a depicted present, then it can be shown that Melancholy had experienced a state of inspiration analagous in profundity to Jerome's and

531. A. Winterstein, "Dürers 'Melancholie I' im Lichte der Psychoanalyse," *Imago, 15* (1929): 145-199; R. Wankmüller-Freyh, "Zu Dürers Kupferstich 'Melencolia'," *Confinia psychiatrica, 3* (1960): 158-169.

[5] As Neoplatonic melancholy: K. Giehlow, "Dürers Stich 'Melencolia I' und der Maximilianische Humanistenkreis," *Mitteilungen der Gesellschaft für Vervielfältigende kunst, 26* (1903): 29-41; *27* (1904): 6-18, 57-78. As tribute to Müller: K. H. de Haas, *Albrecht Dürer's engraving Melencolia I, a symbolic memorial to the scientist Johann Müller* (Rotterdam, 1951). As paradox: P. Reuterswärd, "Sinn und Nebensinn bei Dürer, Randbemerkungen zur 'Melencolia I' " in *Gestalt und Wirklichkeit. Festgabe für Ferdinand Weinhandl,* ed. R. Mühler and J. Fischl (Berlin, 1967), 411-436. And as exhortation: Hoffmann, "Melencolia," 251-277.

[6] E. Panofsky and F. Saxl, *Dürers Kupferstich "Melencolia I"; Eine quellen—und typengeschichtliche Untersuchung* (Leipzig and Berlin, 1923); E. Panofsky, *Dürer, 1:* 154-171; and R. Klibansky, E. Panofsky and F. Saxl, *Saturn and Melancholy* (London, 1964). The general acceptance of Panofsky's ideas is clearly expressed by the publications for and during the Dürer year of 1971; for example, *Albrecht Dürers Umwelt, Festschrift zum 500 Geburtstag,* Nürnberger Forschungen, 15 (Nuremberg, 1971), 154-155; C. Talbot, G. Ravenel and J. Levenson, *Dürer in America. His Graphic Work* (Washington, 1971), 145-146; P. Parshall, "Albrecht Dürer's *St. Jerome in His Study:* A Philological Reference," *Art Bulletin, 53* (1971): 303-305; and R. F. Timken-Zinkann, *Ein Mensch Namens Dürer, Des Künstlers Leben, Ideen, Umwelt* (Berlin, 1972), 107-118.

[7] The numeral I has also been understood as the imperative "ire" (A. Giesecke, "Eine Dürer-Inschrift und ihre richtige Lesung [zu Dürers 'Melancholie'-Stich]," *Gutenberg-Jahrbuch, 30* [1955]: 306-314), as the "fons et origo numerorum" or even the mystical unity of God (P. K. Schuster, "Melencolia I, Studien zu Dürers Melancholiekupferstich und seinem Humanismus," *Das Münster, 27* [1974]: 409-411) and as the shriek of the bat (Reuterswärd, "Melencolia," 414).

[8] Klibansky et al., *Saturn,* 356-357.

[9] For the most cogent refutations of Agrippa as Dürer's source, see K. Rossmann, "Wert und Grenze der Wissenschaft. Zur Symbolik von Dürers Kupferstich 'Melencolia' " in *Offener Horizont. Festschrift für Karl Jaspers* (Munich, 1953), 126-146; and Hoffman, "Melencolia," 251-252.

identical in type to Agrippa's description, but antithetical to the gloomy prospect and spiritual malaise found in the engraving.

THE INSPIRED ACTIVITY OF MELANCHOLY can be demonstrated by a simple, apparently unnoticed, observation: the distance between the points of the compass held by Melancholy is precisely equal to the radius of the sphere at her feet and to one-third of the rainbow's radius measured from the inner edge. While it may be objected that one of the ends of the compass is hidden behind Melancholy's gown thereby rendering any measurement impossible, it nevertheless seems probable that Dürer intended us to make the measurement from the compass points as he depicted them in the engraving. In two preparatory drawings for the engraving (figs. 3 and 4), Dürer devised a similar equation in which the measure indicated by one of the compasses is equal to the length of the base (line 2-3) of the polyhedron and to line 5-6. At first glance, it is tempting to dismiss the identical lengths as coincidental; after all, why would Dürer transfer the measure of the compass on one drawing to the polyhedron on another? While it may have been an accidental correspondence, the probability of this is reduced when one realizes that the base line of the polyhedron is one of the most significant in its construction: it designates one of the planes which truncates the rhomboid, thereby transforming it into the irregular, perplexing object seen in the engraving.[10] Since the presumed correspondence between compass and polyhedron in the drawings was transposed in the engraving to the symbolically crucial compass and sphere, one must wonder whether the repetition of such a precise mathematical conformity can really be mere coincidence.

But could Dürer have expected his public to associate the compass with the radius of the sphere and to reconstruct Melancholy's measurement? If this association would appear recondite, then the frequent depictions of God as the divine geometer (figs. 5 and 6) and of astronomers who measure a sphere with compass should be recalled.[11] Since God created the universe "by measure, number and weight," he was occasionally represented with compass and spheres.[12] The earliest tradition of God as geometer was inspired by the Book of Wisdom and represents him enumerating with the fingers of one hand while holding compass and balances with the other. Unlike the miniatures of the Wisdom type, which neither emphasize the compass over the balance nor represent God using them, another group of miniatures, mostly French, does show God measuring a celestial sphere with compass. The frontispiece to a Bible Moralisé (fig. 5), which may be dated to about 1240, seems to be the earliest, and possible archetype, for this group of illuminations. God, set within a decorative quatrolobe, holds the sphere of the cosmos while placing the two points of his compass at the center and circumference. The particular choice of center and circumference, duplicated later by Dürer's Melancholy, is repeated not only in the antecedents to this manuscript but also in illuminations from the early fifteenth-century of the *Historia Scholastica* such as that by Guyart des Moulins (fig. 6).

Such examples suggest that the act of measurement, and by implication its reconstruction, was an accepted fragment of the contem-

[10] For the geometrical formulation of the polyhedron, see O. Zedlitz, "Nochmals: Der 'Kristall' auf Dürers Stich 'Melencolia I'," *Forschungen und Fortschritte, 33* (1959): 154-156; and Klibansky et al., *Saturn*, 400-403.

[11] For astronomers, see Hans Brosamer in *Astronomicum Caesarcum* (Ingolstadt, 1540), an anonymous woodcut in A. Niphus, *De liberatione a metu futuri dituvii* (Venice, 1523) and illus. in G. Hellmann, *Beiträge zur Geschichte der Meteorologie* (Berlin, 1914), 83; the title page of *Messahala de scientia motus orbis* (Nuremberg, 1504) by an artist from Dürer's circle (illus. in F. W. Hollstein, *German Engravings Etchings and Woodcuts* [Amsterdam, 1960], *7:* 257); and Cornelius Massys' woodcut of *Saturn* as astronomer, which is derived from Dürer's *Melencolia* (illus. in Hollstein, *Dutch and Flemish Etchings Engravings and Woodcuts* [Amsterdam, 1955], *2:* 198).

[12] Klibansky et al., *Saturn*, 338f.; J. B. Friedman, "The Architect's Compass in Creation Miniatures of the Later Middle Ages," *Traditio, 30* (1974): 419-429.

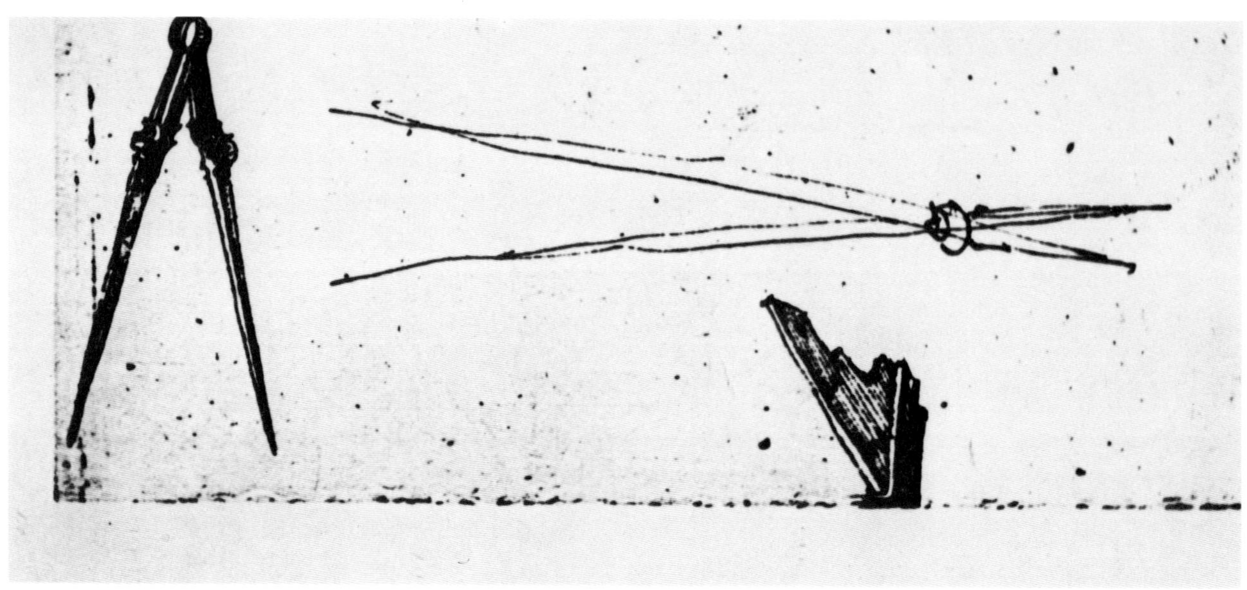

Fig. 3. Albrecht Dürer, Compasses *(detail), c. 1514. Pen and ink. Sächsische Landesbibliothek, Dresden. The dimensions of the full drawing are 20.0 x 26.0 cm ($7\frac{7}{8}$ x $10\frac{1}{4}$ in)*

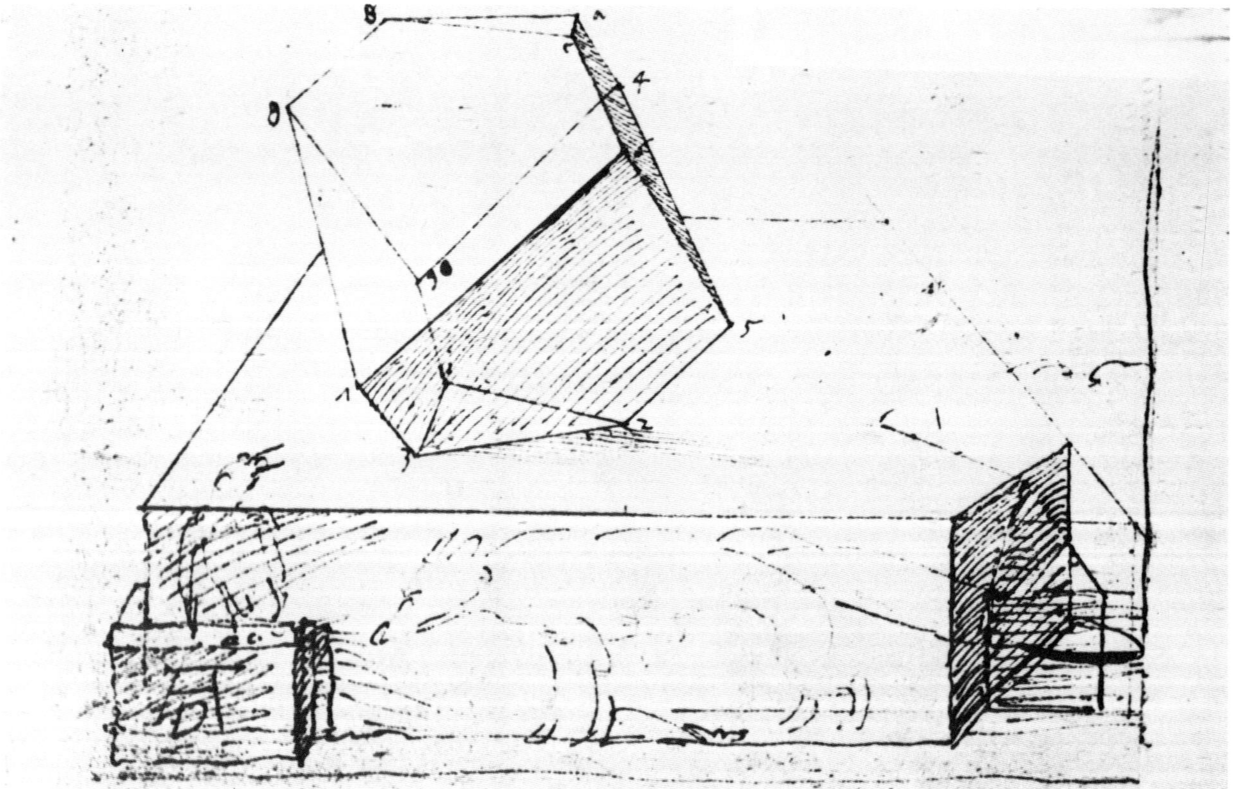

Fig. 4. Albrecht Dürer, Polyhedron *(detail), c. 1514. Pen and ink. Sächsische Landesbibliothek, Dresden. The dimensions of the full drawing are 20.2 x 19.3 cm ($7\frac{15}{16}$ x $7\frac{5}{8}$ in)*

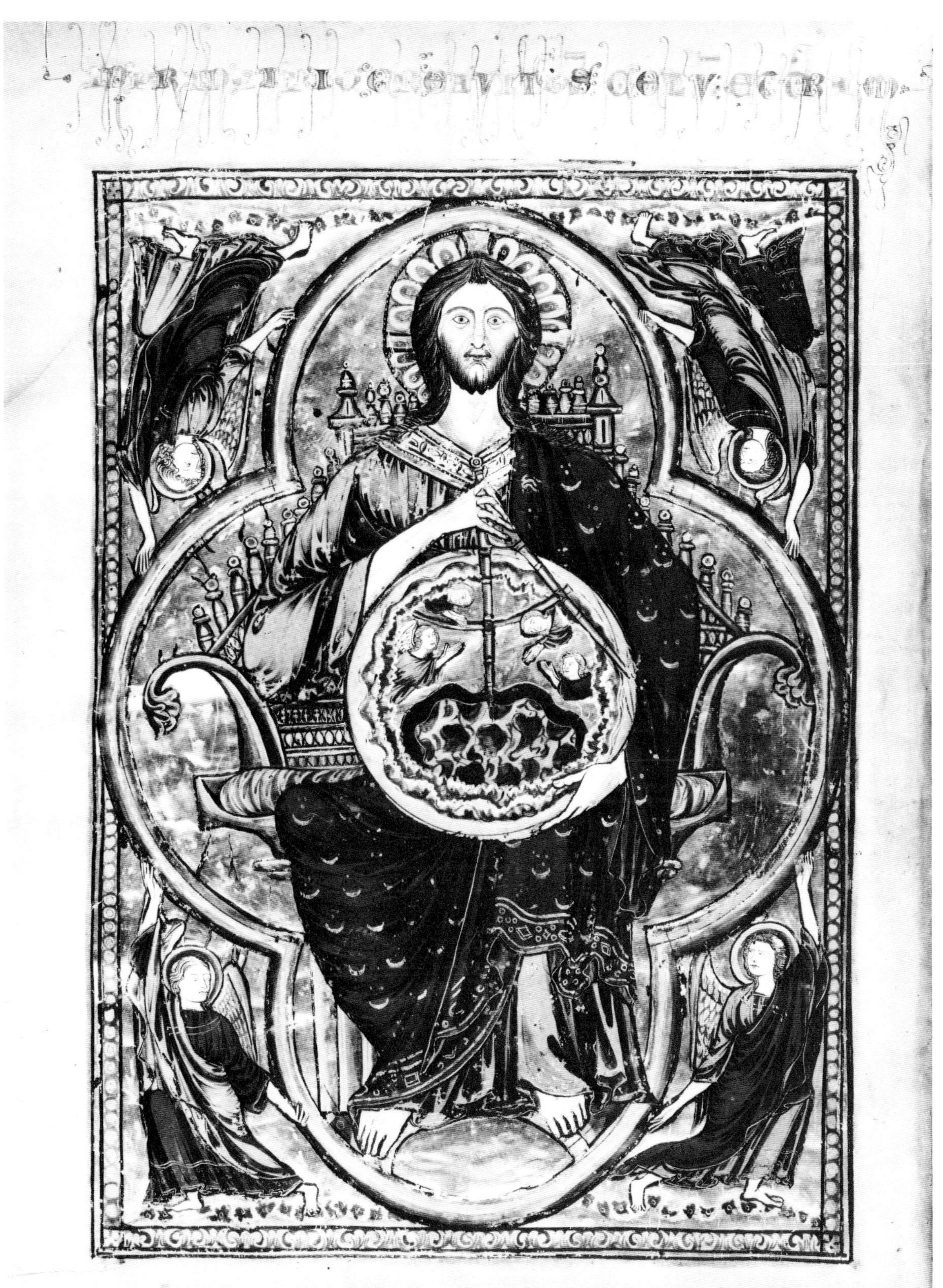

Fig. 5. God the Father with Sphere and Compass, *c. 1240. From the Bible Moralisé. Bodleian Library, Oxford, 270b, fol. 1*

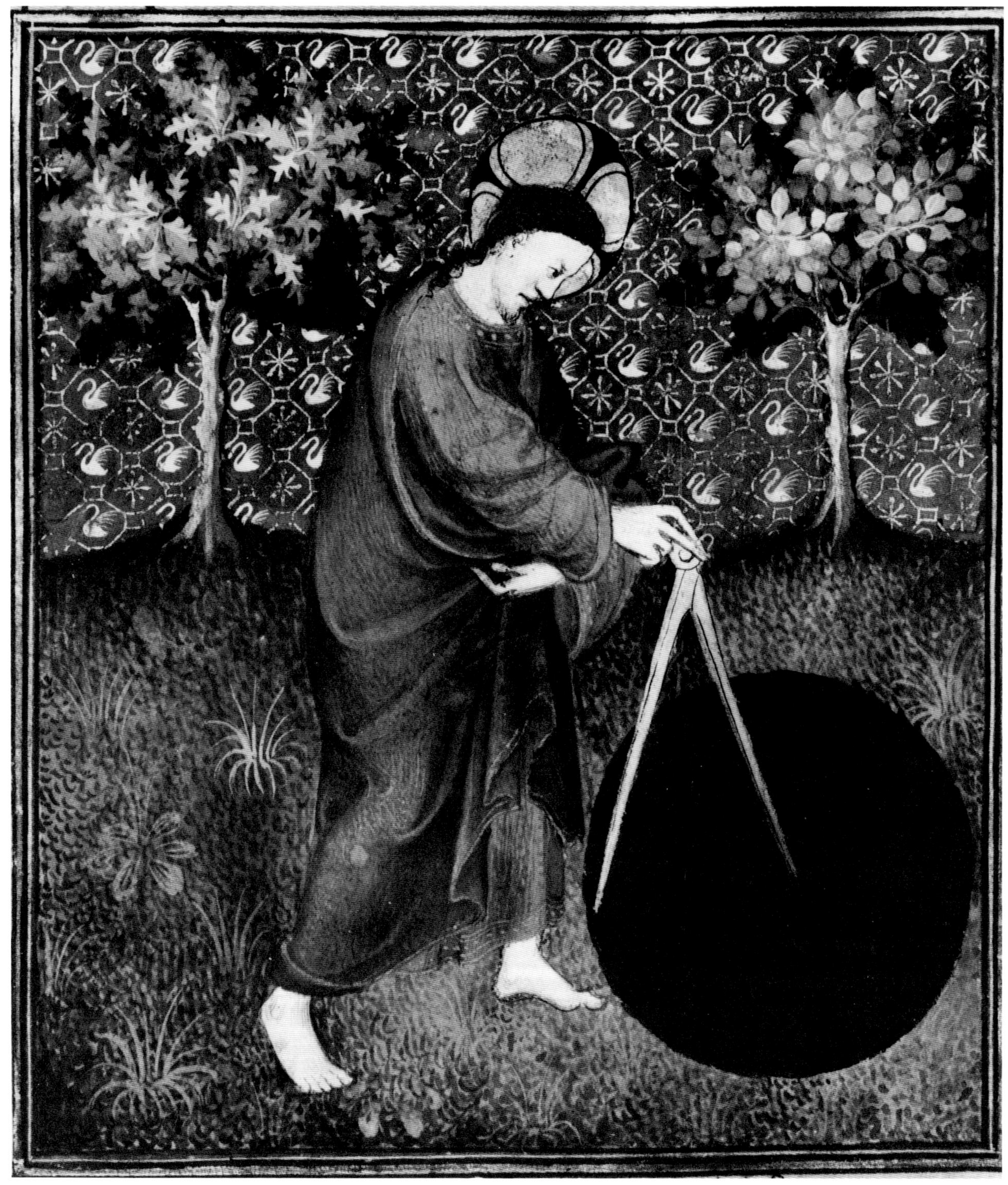

Fig. 6. God the Father with Sphere and Compass, *early 15th c. From Guyart des Moulins,* Historia Scholastica. *British Library, London, 15.D.iii, fol. 3v*

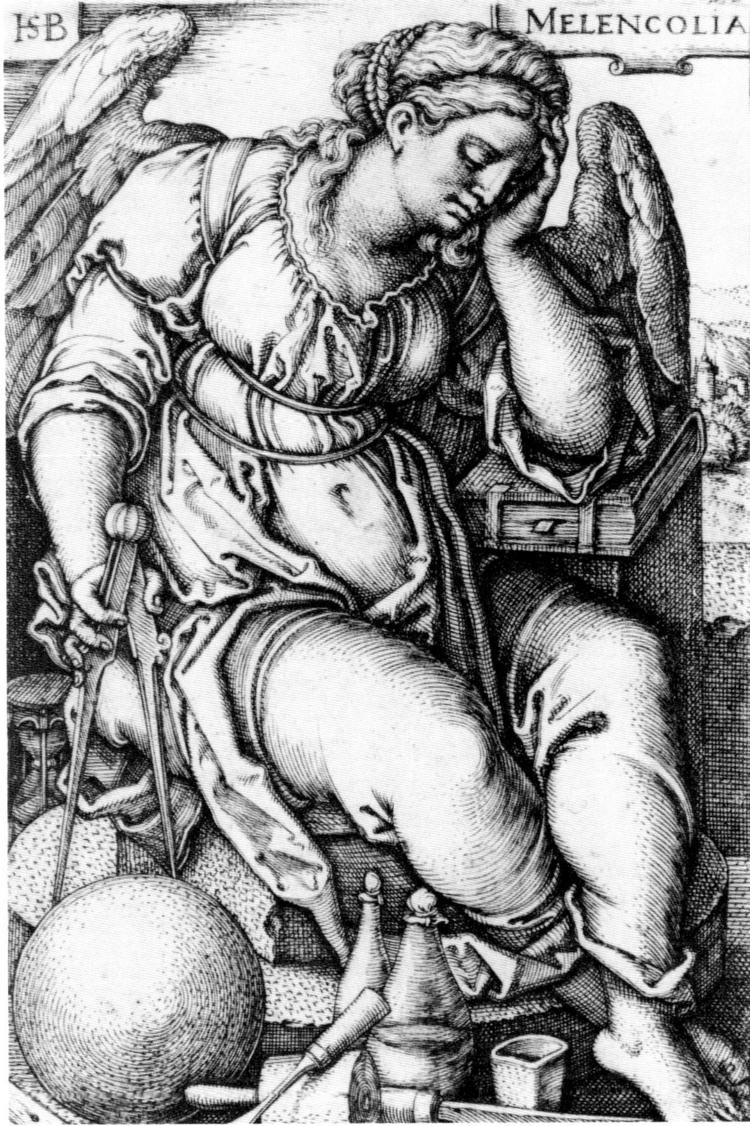

Fig. 7. Hans Beham, Melencolia, *1539. Engraving. National Gallery of Art, Washington, Rosenwald Collection*

porary visual memory. Hence Dürer might well have intended his learned audience to reconstruct the prior act of Melancholy in gauging the radius of the sphere, and in fact, at least one of Dürer's colleagues did just that. Hans Beham's engraving of *Melancholy* (fig. 7) dated 1539, which is clearly derived from Dürer, depicts a winged woman resting her compass on top of a sphere whose radius equals the distance between the points of the compass.[13]

The simple, mathematical unity of the compass, sphere, and rainbow in *Melencolia I* has significant implications, but, to arrive at them, the meaning of the sphere and rainbow must first be understood. The sphere is one of the most malleable symbols, and for this reason it is the bane of iconographers.[14] In *Melencolia I* it has been interpreted as a symbol of the earth, of unstability or *fortuna,* and of pure geometry.[15] The rainbow has been interpreted as the upper-

[13] Later, Cesare Ripa (*Iconologia* [Rome, 1603], 308) represented Mathematics as a winged woman holding a celestial sphere in one hand and compass in the other. Again the radius of the sphere is indicated by the compass.

[14] O. Brendel, "Symbolik der Kugel," *Mitteilungen des deutschen archaeologischen Instituts, Rom* (Abteilung, li, 1936), *51:* 1-95.

[15] As symbol of earth, see J. Kappel, "Die Sinndeutung in Dürers Melencolia," *Christliche Kunst, 24* (1927-1928): 211-212; as fortune, see F. Nagel, *Der Kristall auf Dürers Melancholie* (Nuremberg, 1922), 12; Schuster, "Melencolia," 409; Reuterswärd, "Melencolia," 416. For a broader discussion of the sphere as a vanity sumbol, see L. Möller, "Die Kugel als Vanitassymbol," *Jahrbuch der Hamburger Kunstsammlungen, 2*

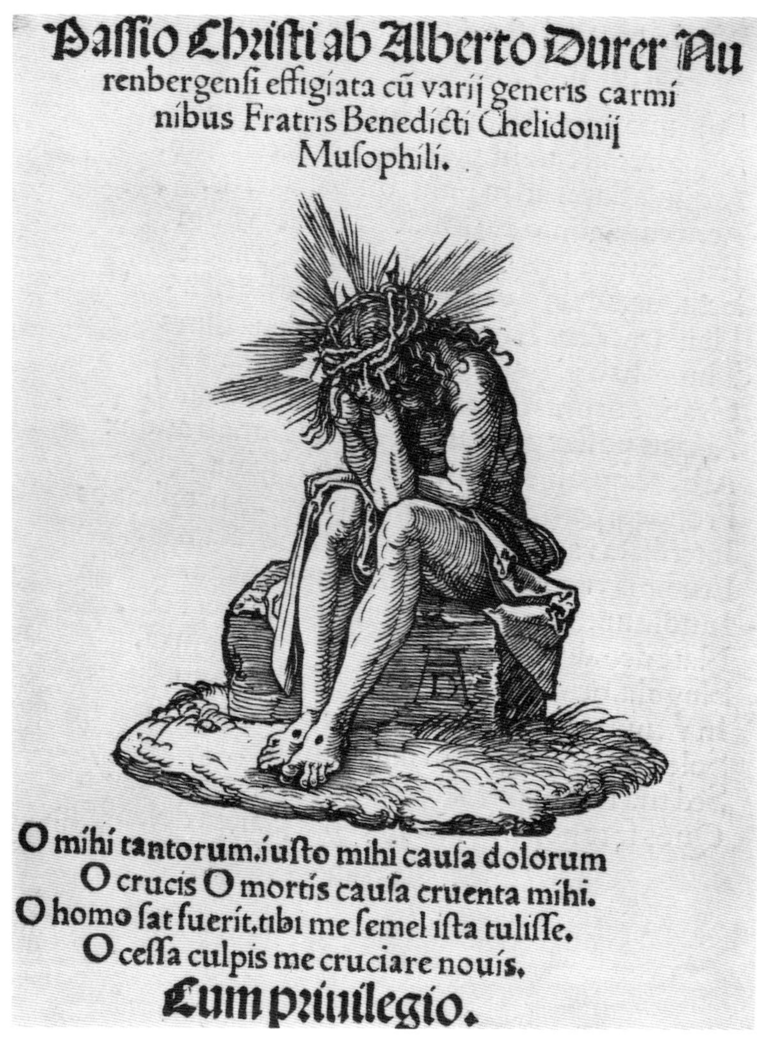

Fig. 8. Albrecht Dürer, Man of Sorrows Seated, *1511. Woodcut. The Brooklyn Museum, New York, Gift of Mrs. Howard M. Morse*

most, heavenly sphere within the Neoplatonic system, as a divine assurance after the Flood, and as an indication of the melancholic's prognostic powers.[16] However, when it is recognized that the sphere and rainbow are proportionally related and should be interpreted together rather than separately, a different context is established: that of the Last Judgment. The rainbow and sphere maintain the hieratic order and meaning of Christ's throne and footstool in most scenes of the Last Judgment.[17] The interpretation of the rainbow as a symbol of the celestial order is also implied by its Latin designation *arcus caelestis* and is stated by Gregory in his eighth Homilia.[18] The sphere would then assume its conventional meaning as a symbol of the earth.

The reference to the Last Judgment is echoed by the scales on the wall in *Melencolia I*, and its meaning is amplified by the tools on the ground and the objects on the wall. While the tools scattered on the ground have usually been thought to define the realm of Melancholy's gift, Reutersward has perceived a coexisting substratum of sym-

(1952): 161ff.; and Franz Bächtiger, *Vanitas-Schicksalsdeutung in der deutschen Renaissance-graphik*, Inaugural Dissertation (Munich, 1970), 72-88. For the bell as a symbol of transience, see Giehlow, "Melencholia," 65. As symbol of geometry, see Klibansky et al., *Saturn*, 328.

[16] For the rainbow as heavenly sphere, see R. W. Horst, "Dürers 'Melencolia I'. Beitrag zum Melancholeia-Problem," *Wandlungen Christlicher Kunst im Mittelalter* (Forschungen zur Kunstgeschichte und Christlichen Archäologie), 2 (1953): 426-427. As divine assurance, see Hoffmann, "Melencolia," 258-259; and as an indication of prognostic powers, see Klibansky et al., *Saturn*, 360.

[17] S. Rösch, "Der Regenbogen in der Malerei," *Studium Generale, 13* (1960): 422-423; Craig Harbison, *The Last Judgment in Sixteenth-Century Northern Europe* (New York, 1976).

[18] J. P. Migne, *Patrologiae Latina, 76:* 867-868: "Sed si ipsi quam praediximus visioni arcus inten-

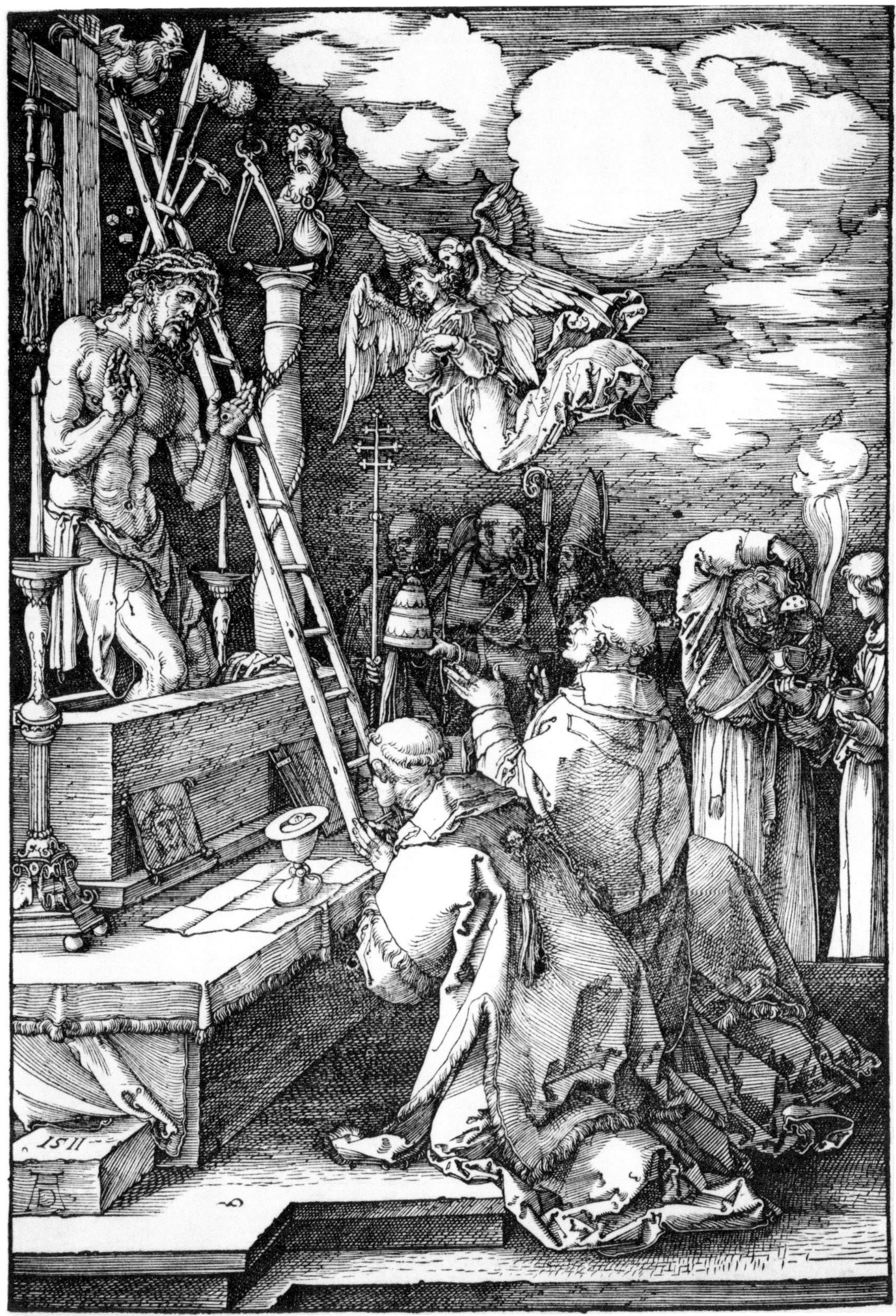

Fig. 9. Albrecht Dürer, The Mass of St. Gregory, *1511. Woodcut. National Gallery of Art, Washington, Rosenwald Collection*

dimus, quomodo arcus significet spiritum videmus" ("But if we turn our attention to the vision itself of the rainbow, which we related before, we see how the rainbow signifies the spirit").

[19] Reutersward, "Melencolia," 411-436.

bolism.[19] His point of departure was the observation that a skull may be dimly discerned on the main facet of the polyhedron. Whether one can accept this image as a skull is of less importance than his suggestion that the objects surrounding Melancholy may be interpreted in similar terms. While Panofsky considered the hourglass and bell as symbols of the measure of time, Reutersward noted that they could also be allusions to the passage of time and therefore to death. The comet may refer to the melancholic's forecasting ability, but at the same time it can serve as a symbol of death. The sphere as a symbol of the earth could be identified with the image of earth frequently depicted as Fortuna's unstable base. The nails, saw, hammer, and ladder refer not just to death and fortune in general but specifically to Christ's Passion. The pose of Melancholy herself alludes to Christ as the Man of Sorrows: indeed these images could almost have been transferred anagramatically from Dürer's woodcut of that subject and the Mass of St. Gregory (figs. 8, 9).[20]

[20] H. von Einem ("Notes on Dürer's 'Melencolia I'," *Print Review*, 5 [1976]: 35-39) associates the pose of Melancholy with Dürer's Job in the Heller Altarpiece and the titlepage woodcut of the Small Passion thereby imputing a Christian content to the engraving. J. A. Endres ("Albrecht Dürer und Nikolaus von Kusa. Deutung der Dürerschen 'Melancholie'," *Die Christliche Kunst*, 9 [1912-1913]: 110-120) in one of the few other interpretations of Melencolia as a Christian allegory suggests that the magic square in adding up to thirty-four could refer both to the age of Christ during the Passion and to Cusa's thirty-fourth sphere.

Although the interpretations of the tools and instruments as symbols of the realm of *melancholia imaginativa* and of the Passion and *vanitas* would seem to be mutually exclusive, it can be shown that Dürer planned disparate ideas to coincide within a single object. But before Panofsky's and Reutersward's ideas can be reconciled and elaborated on, the significance of the sphere-rainbow relationship must be returned to.

If the sphere and rainbow do allude to the Last Judgment and consequently to the earth and prismatic arch of Heaven, then the proportional relationship between them probably refers to Pythagoras' renowned theory that earth and Heaven, or microcosm and macrocosm, are related by number.[21] Indeed the implication of celestial and terrestrial harmony is even contained within the meaning of a rainbow, since it served as God's sign of covenant to Noah after the Flood (Genesis 9:12-15). Certainly the one to three ratio of sphere to rainbow is a gross simplification of Pythagorian ideas; nevertheless, it could serve as a lucid symbol for the greater mathematical order of the universe. If this can be accepted, then several conclusions may be drawn.

[21] R. Allers, "Microcosmos from Anaximandros to Paracelsus," *Traditio*, 2 (1944): 319-408; L. Spitzer, "Classical and Christian Ideas of World Harmony," *Traditio*, 2 (1944): 409-464; Dietrich Mahnke, *Unendliche Sphäre und Allmittelpunkt* (Stuttgart, 1966); and Heinz Meyer, *Die Zahlenallegorese im Mittelalter* (Munich, 1975), 67ff. Dürer could have become acquainted with these ideas from a variety of sources, possibly from Bovillus (*Liber de Sapiente* [Augsburg, 1510], chap. 30) or Luca Pacioli (*De Divina Proportione* [Venice, 1509], pt. 1, chaps. 1-6).

In measuring the earth, and by extension the Heavens, Melancholy has demonstrated her knowledge of geometry and thus confirms her Saturnine gifts, as Panofsky postulated. Presumably, Melancholy obtained the measure of the world to apply it to her architectural project, thereby incorporating the same principles used by God when he created the universe "by measure, number and weight." According to Pythagoras, each celestial sphere emits a different tone according to its velocity, and these tones are harmonically, that is proportionally, related to the whole. For this reason musical proportion was thought to be the essential organizational principle of the universe and could be translated into architecture, as Melancholy presumably intended to do, to create a terrestrial model of Heaven.[22] Indeed Melancholy's lofty aspirations are confirmed by the fact that the act of measuring the sphere recalls popular images of God as the divine geometer or architect of the cosmos.

[22] Otto von Simson, *The Gothic Cathedral* (London, 1956), 21ff.; Hermann Graf, *Bibliographie zum Problem der Proportionen. Literatur über Proportionen, Mass und Zahl in Architektur, Bildender Kunst und Natur* (Speyer, 1958).

The decision to represent God measuring a sphere with compass was suggested by the metaphorical conception of him as the architect of the universe creating order from chaos, by means of number.

During the Renaissance, the metaphor of God as artificer was inverted so that the artist or architect could also be considered divine. This inversion of a medieval formula, so typical of the age of humanism, was understood and propounded by Dürer, who thought the equation of the artist with God perfectly natural since both ordered form by means of geometry.[23] It was probably for this reason that Dürer chose to recall the medieval illuminations of God as geometer with his Melancholy. Thus, in this respect, Melancholy may be seen as the imitator of God and hence a perfect illustration of Agrippa's *furor divinus*.

Yet, despite her apparently successful grasp of the universal harmony, Melancholy is represented as inactive and dejected, and not as elated and prepared to pursue her remarkable achievement. The reasons for her dejection may be found in a recurrent theme in Western thought, certainly known to Dürer—the futility of scientific pursuit. As I have indicated in the introduction, scholars have generally recognized that the complex iconography of *Melencolia I* revolves around the peculiar gifts of the melancholic, gifts which inevitably preclude him from participating in the fulfillment of divine wisdom.[24] In a passage recognized by Panofsky to be a significant part of Melencolia's heritage, the thirteenth-century philosopher Henricus de Gandavo defined the two types of thinkers.[25] According to Henricus, some men are able to handle metaphysical concepts, and hence become theologians, while others are limited to perceptible reality and quantifiable existence and hence are ideally suited to become scientists. These people cannot transcend the concrete quantities of time and space and, in the words of Henricus, "therefore such men are melancholy, and become excellent mathematicians but very bad metaphysicians, for they cannot extend their thoughts beyond location and space."

In the search for Dürer's sources, one important text has been neglected—Sebastian Brant's *Ship of Fools*. Brant's compilation of medieval morality, which ridicules in pithy verse the foibles of most earthly pursuits, grew out of a well-established anti-rationalist tradition which was initially defined by Sextus Empericus. This tradition survived through the Middle Ages, despite the challenges of Abelard and Aquinas, to lucidly articulated during the fifteenth-century by Nicholas of Cusa.[26] Wisdom, or knowledge of God, for Cusa was infinite and thus "unutterable in any words, unintelligible to any intellect, unmeasurable by any measure, . . . unproportionable by any proportion."[27] In short, divine wisdom could not be approached through reason or the senses; in fact, reason could divert one's attention to the false, and because of this, Cusa propounded his most famous paradox, that of learned ignorance. The humble and ignorant, for Cusa, are able to appreciate the mystical infinity of divine wisdom because they are not blinkered by the strictures of worldly knowledge. The ideas of Cusa, and the tradition on which he modeled his thoughts, found fertile ground in the mind of Martin Luther: "Those therefore who are wise in and concerning visible things . . . understand nothing and are wise in nothing, that is, they are neither intelligent nor wise, but foolish and blind. And though they may think themselves wise men, yet they have become fools, for they are wise, not in the wisdom of secret, hidden things, but of that

[23] One year before his *Melencolia*, Dürer wrote: "This great art of painting has been held in high esteem by the mighty kings many hundred years ago. They made the outstanding artists rich and treated them with distinction because they felt that the great masters had an equality with God, as it is written. For, a good painter is inwardly full of figures, and if it were possible for him to live on forever he would always have to pour forth something new from the inner ideas of which Plato writes." Panofsky, *Dürer*, 280.

[24] Panofsky relates it to Dürer's later disillusionment with geometry as a means to perfect beauty (Panofsky, *Dürers Kunsttheorie*, [Berlin, 1915], 127f.; Panofsky, *Dürer*, 171). He cites such passages from the artist's notes as "With regard to geometry, one can prove that certain things are true, but certain things one must leave to the opinion and judgment of men." Whether Dürer felt a comparable doubt concerning geometry in the earlier years of *Melencolia* cannot be accepted without questioning his sincerity in composing his treatise, the *Underweysung der Messung mit dem Zirckel und Richtscheyt*, which was prepared during these years, but published in 1525. His sentiment concerning the role of geometry in art is expressed in a note which probably does not date later than 1513: "ist keine, dy der mass mer vnd jn manigfeltiger weg vnd gestalt notturfftig ist als dy kunst der malerey, dy nit alain begert des geometrei vnd arithmetica, vrsprung aller mass, sunder vil mer der ander kunst des betrugs des gesicht, catoptrica, geodesia, chorographia"; see Rupprich, *Nachlass*, 2: 127.

[25] Panofsky, *Dürer*, 168.

[26] The scepticism of Cusa, which also derives from the mystics Eckhart, Lull and the Brethren of the Common Life, may be traced back to Pseudo-Dionysius and the school of Chartres and ultimately to such Pauline passages as: "For wisdom of this world is foolishness to God" (I Corinthians 3:19); see E. Rice, "Nicholas of Cusa's Idea of Wisdom," *Traditio*, *13* (1957): 345-368; and Anton Lübke, *Nikolaus von Kues, Kirchenfürst zwischen Mittelalter und Neuzeit* (Munich, 1968), 276-292.

[27] Cusa, *De sapientia ignorata*, 9-10; see also E. Grant, "Nicole Oresme and the Commensurability or Incommensurability of the Celestial Motions," *Archive for History of Exact Sciences*, *1* (1961): 420-458.

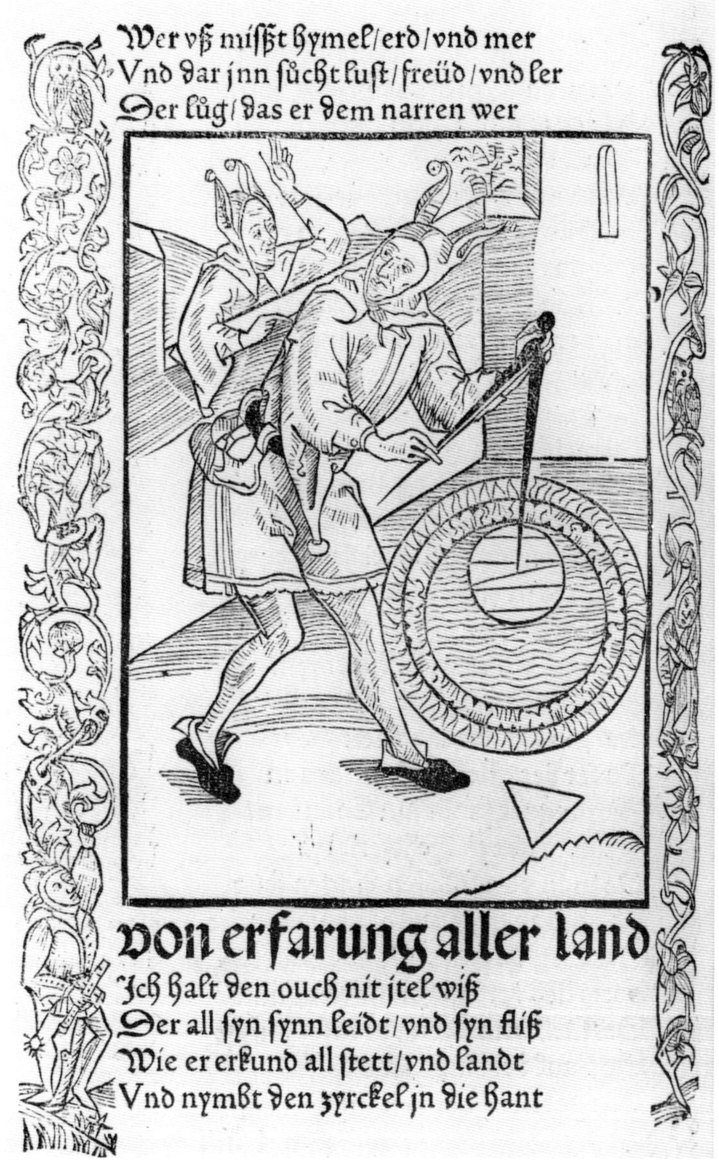

Fig. 10. Sebastian Brant, Narrenschiff *(Basel, 1494), chap. 66*

which can be found in a human way."[28] The shattering doubts raised by Luther concerning the role of the Church were paralleled by a general intellectual unrest, not only in such religious leaders but also by such secular thinkers as Giovanni Francesco Pico della Mirandola, the nephew of the renowned Giovanni Pico, Agrippa von Nettesheim, and Faustino Perisauli.[29] Whereas Cusa and Luther limited their scepticism of reason to theology, with occasional excursions into other fields of learning by way of comparison, the emergent neo-Pyrrhonists questioned the validity of all human knowledge since it must be based on the deceptive senses. This position, derived from Sextus' *Outlines of Pyrrhonism,* undermined the assumptions of the sciences not simply as a means for understanding eternal, divine truths but also within its own limited context of quantifiable phenomena.[30]

[28] Luther, *Werke* (Weimar, 1938), *56:* 237. The Pauline Epistles certainly inspired Luther on this theme, but Jacques Lefèvre d'Etaples might also have been influential; see P. Imbart de la Tour, *Les Origines de la Réforme* (Paris, 1903-1935), *2:* 566-568.

[29] For a general review of their ideas, see Richard Popkin, *The History of Scepticism from Erasmus to Descartes* (Assen, 1960), 17-25; Charles Nauert, *Agrippa and the Crisis of Renaissance Thought* (Urbana, Ill., 1965), 148-152; Charles Schmitt, *Gianfrancesco Pico della Mirandola (1469-1533) and his Critique of Aristotle* (The Hague, 1967), 49-51, 75-81; and Faustino Perisauli, *De Triumpho Stultitiae,* ed. G. Fabbri with intro. by A. Viviani (Florence, 1963).

[30] Within the context of the deception of the senses, it might be significant that at least two physicians of

As a pure science and one of the liberal arts, geometry and its applications in astronomy and geography became an inclusive image of scientific vanity. Augustine devoted two chapters of his *Confessions* (Book 5:3-4) to the astronomer's misplaced faith in measurement. Erasmus, in his parade of pompous fools, included scientists and astronomers, remarking: "They announce that they alone are wise, and that the rest of men are only passing shadows. Their folly is a pleasant one. They frame countless worlds, and measure the sun, moon, stars, and spheres as with thumb and line."[31] Agrippa introduced his treatise *De incertitudine et vanitate omnium scientiarum et artium liber,* published in 1530, with a critique of reason and its limited applicability. He continued by dismissing mathematics and geometry, as well as such dependent disciplines as astronomy, geography, and even painting, as being utterly vain and ultimately harmful. In a passage recalling that by Henricus de Gandavo, Agrippa wrote: "and therefore, while they (the geometricians) go about still adding something which their Masters left Imperfect, they run themselves into such an extremity of Madness, which all the Hellebore in the world is not able to Purge away."[32] Pico and Perisauli denounce geometry and astronomy in similar terms, and several sixteenth-century German woodcuts translated this theme into images.[33] While it might appear unlikely that Dürer shared these ideas, at least in view of various depreciatory comments about the sceptics,[34] it should be remembered that his thoughts might have taken a more pessimistic turn with the death of his mother in 1514, an experience which profoundly affected the artist and possibly influenced his conception of the contemporary *Melencolia.*[35]

Sebastian Brant's *Ship of Fools,* published in 1494, stands in the early phase of the anti-intellectual, Pyrrhonist revival and seems to have served as an important source for Dürer's *Melencolia I.*[36] Brant assembled a compendium of vain attempts at mundane pleasures, fame, riches, and knowledge to serve as a satiric foil for his primary theme—the blindness of mankind to its ultimate fate.[37] The sixty-sixth chapter, "Of Experience of All Lands," deals with the vanity of mundane knowledge, specifically the measurement of the earth and heavens as a sterile means to understand the universe. The introductory verse provides the theme of the chapter: "Who measures heaven, earth, and sea,/ Thus seeking lore or gaiety,/ Let him beware a fool to be."[38] The opening lines of the chapter restate the theme in more complete form:

I do not deem him very wise
Who energetically tries
To probe all cities, every land,
And takes compass well in hand
That thereby he may well decide
How broad the earth, how long and wide,
How deep and large the seas expand,
What holds th'extremest sphere of land.[39]

The woodcut which introduces this chapter represents a fool using a compass to measure the earth, which is surrounded by the heavens (fig. 10). The fool has placed one point of the compass in the center of the earth and waits to move the other arm while he listens to the admonitions of a wise fool, who indicates the nature of his advice by

the sixteenth century, Leonard Fuchs and Ianus Matthaeus Durastantes, observed that the condition of melancholy could result in unreliable sensory perception; see L. Fuchs, *De curandi ratione* (Lyons, 1548), bk. 1, chaps. 29-34; and L. Thorndike, *History of Magic* (New York, 1941), *6:* 517-519.

[31] Erasmus, *In Praise of Folly,* trans. L. Dean (Chicago, 1946), 94-95.

[32] Agrippa, *The Vanity of Arts and Sciences* (London, 1684), chap. 22; Agrippa, *De incertitudine et vanitate omnium scientiarum et artium liber* (1530; Antwerp, 1643), chap. 22: "Ea tamen est eorum ambitio, ut priorum traditionibus nunquam acquiescant, sed in talibus amplius aliquid quam magistri eorum invenire putantes, seipsos in tantam insaniam agunt quam universae terrae elleborum non sufficiat expurgare ab ipsa Geometria ultra hoc . . . ."

[33] G. F. Pico della Mirandola, *Examen vanitatis doctrinae gentium et veritatis Christianae, disciplinae* (Mirandola, 1520), chap. 16; Perisauli, *Triumpho Stultitiae,* chap. 10 "Geometra Delirus" and chap. 11 "Astronomia Mera Insania." Matthias Gerung, in his woodcut the *Melancholic,* depicts a geographer measuring a terrestrial sphere with compass and indicates the work as sterile with the inscription: "Las Iecr Gheta I. FNDI, Hat 1z Baczen versplit" (illus. in G. F. Hartlaub, *Giorgiones Geheimnis* [Munich, 1925], pl. 27). In a slightly later woodcut, of about 1548, Heinrich Vogtherr the Elder shows an astronomer posed melancholically with head on hand and identifies the source of his lethargy thus: "Azarchel hat dweltzung der Zat/ Beschriben gmachet offenbar/ Die rechnung ist im gsyn erfande/ Der zircel dlingen ouch verwandt" (illus. in M. Geisberg, *The German Single-Leaf Woodcut, 1500-1550* [New York, 1974], *4:* 1385). The astronomer in Breughel's drawing and engraving of *Temperance* seems to be indulging in an intemperate activity as are those around him; see C. de Tolnay, *Die Zeichnungen Pieter Bruegels* (Munich, 1925), 27 f., 63f.; and I. Zupnick, "Bruegel's *Virtues* as the Epitomy of Folly" in *L'Umanesimo e "la Follia"* (Rome, 1971), 91-106. In particular, the precarious position of the astronomer measuring the heavens, in comparison to the more stable grounding of the geographer, possibly alludes to the vanity of that discipline.

[34] "Aber vnser blöd gemüt kan zw solcher volkumenheit aller künstn, warheit vnd weisheit nit kumen. Doch sind wir nit gar awsgeschlossen van aller weisheit. Wöll wir durch lernung unser vernunft scherpfen vnd vns dorin ỹben, so mügen wir woll etlich warheit durch recht weg suchen, lernen, erlangen, erkennen vnd dort zw dumen. Wir wissen, daz jr vill mencherlëy kunst erfaren vn jr warheit angetzeight haben, das vns zw gut kumt. Dorum ist es billich, das sich der mensch nit versawn vnd zw bekwemer tzeit etwas leren, dortzw er sich am aller geschicktesten find. Etlich menschen mügen van allerlëy künsten lernen, aber daz ist nit einem jtlichen geben. Doch ist kein vernunftig mensch so grob, er mag etwan ein ding lernen, dortzw jn sein gemüt am höchsten tregt"; see Rupprich, *Nachlass, 2:* 112. See also H. Schrade, "Die religiösen Grundlagen von Dürers Schriften zur Kunst," *Zeitschrift für dt. Bildung, 10* (1934): 22-29; and G. Weise, *Dürer*

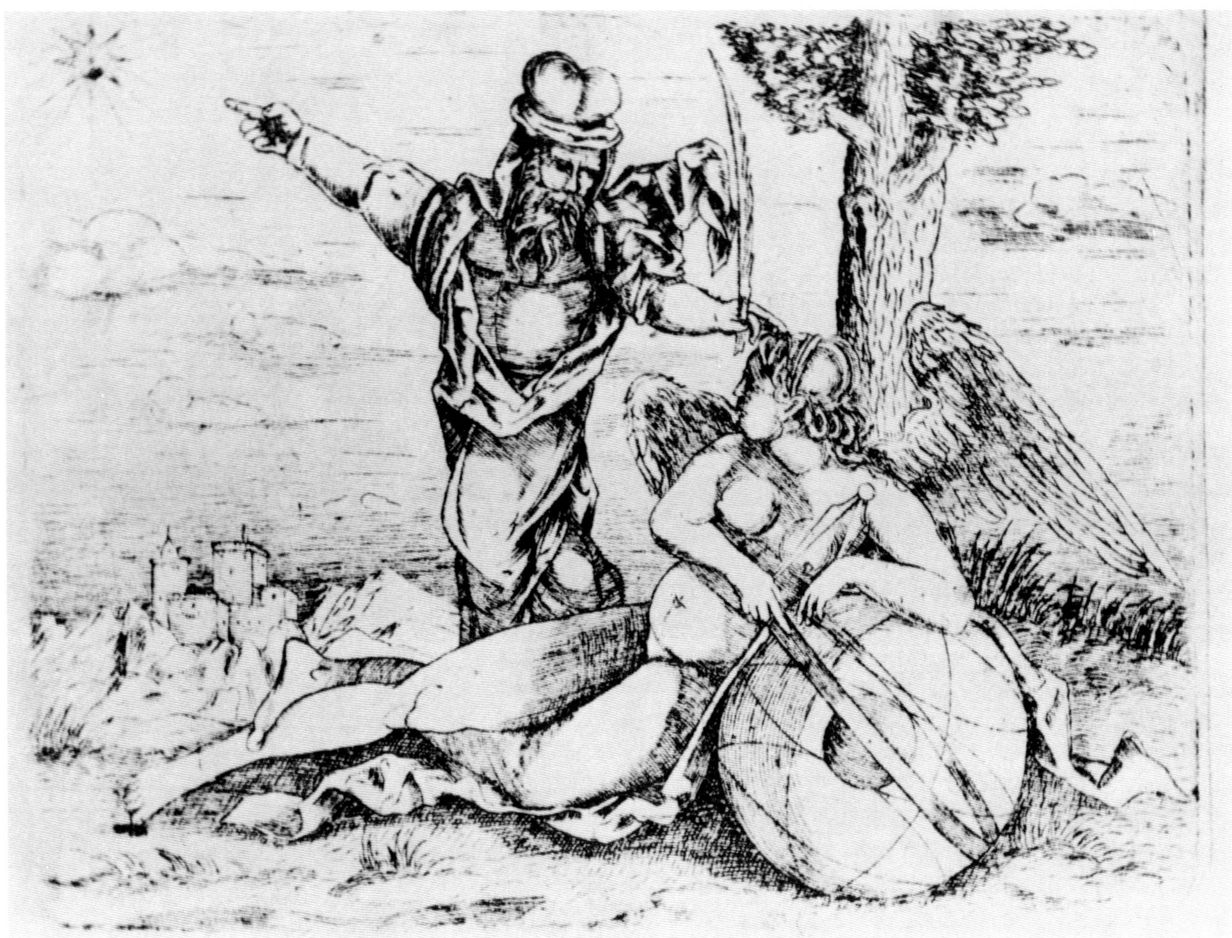

Fig. 11. Attributed to the Master of 1515, Allegory of Astronomy. *Engraving. The Albertina, Vienna*

und die Ideale der Humanisten, Tübinger Forschungen zur Kunstgeschichte 6 (Tübingen, 1953), 8-16, 28-33.

[35] Rupprich, *Nachlass, 1:* 37; R. Wustmann, "Als Dürers Mutter starb," *Kunstchronik, 14* (1902-1903): 425-430. See also W. Waetzoldt, *Dürer und seine Zeit* (Vienna, 1935), 239; and Donald Kuspit, "Dürer and the Northern Critics, 1502-1572," Ph.D. diss., University of Michigan, 1971, 235-276.

[36] That Dürer was familiar with the *Ship of Fools* cannot be doubted since he designed many of its woodcuts while he was in Basel, probably from mid-1492 until the fall of 1493; see F. Winkler, *Dürer und die Illustrationen zum Narrenschiff* (Berlin, 1951); and H. Lüdecke, *Albrecht Dürers Wanderjahre* (Dresden, 1959). Although Dürer was not responsible for the woodcut of Chapter 66, he certainly must have known it. M. Lemmer (*Die Holzschnitte zu Sebastian Brants Narrenschiff* [Leipzig, 1964], 149) attributes the woodcut to the "Gnad-her-Meister" whose style he characterizes as movemented and expressive, often to an excess of bestial terror rendered without subtlety. Brant's influence on the iconography of Dürer's work, in particular the *Dream of the Doctor,* has been discussed

pointing to the text above. The act of measuring the world corresponds closely to the earlier activity of Dürer's Melancholy.

Brant, relying on the sceptical tradition, elucidates the folly implicit in this attempt and characteristically infuses into it a medieval morality. By measuring the universe, the fool has attempted to transcend his natural limits: "Why should we humans seek to be/More than we are in verity?"[40] Inspired Melancholy, who has measured the earth like Brant's fool, tried to be "more than we are in verity"; in other words, she aspired to imitate God as the divine geometer. And in the process of hoping to understand God through geometry, and even become like God, Melancholy, like Brant's geographer, entered a realm which she could not understand, and therefore she neglected those matters which have eternal importance. Brant, in the sixty-sixth chapter, wrote of his fool:

The master Pliny once did say
That vain it is in every way
To measure out the world's expanse
And then to cast a further glance
Beyond the earth, beyond the sea;
In this all men err grievously,
Into these problems each would delve,

Yet can he understand himself? . . .
We never know what gain it brings
To study many lofty things,
No one his hour of dying knows,
Which like a shadow comes and goes.[41]

These might well be the thoughts of Melancholy as she casts "a further glance beyond the earth, beyond the sea." By vainly seeking to understand the world by means of geometry, she does not recognize her own mortality, a theme also stressed by Augustine and later by Agrippa and others.[42] Thus Brant's text confirms Reutersward's hypothesis that Dürer included the themes of vanity and mortality in his engraving.[43]

Melencolia I has usually been interpreted as a timeless emblem filled with static symbols,[44] but with the discovery of Melancholy's act of measuring the sphere, a past and present can be unequivocably defined. The abandoned tools, the unfinished building, and, most importantly, the compass bearing the measure of the sphere indicate a past state of activity, one which has already been identified with Agrippa's *furor melancholicus*. If the flights of the comet and the bat as well as the appearance of the rainbow are considered as natural phenomena rather than just timeless symbols, then they represent a restricted span of time, specifically the present moment. The sequence of time implicitly contained in the engraving suggests a dramatic narrative which focuses on the transformation of Melancholy's mood from inspired melancholy to the inactive and dejected state depicted in the engraving. Since the specific moment in time in which the transformation of Melancholy's awareness occurs is defined by the principal temporal phenomena—the comet, the rainbow, and the flying bat—they acquire a greater importance than generally assumed. Indeed the significance of Melancholy's depression is conveyed primarily by means of the temporal imagery.

The comet, as a traditional symbol of death and impending misfortune, can be understood as a *memento mori* and, in the context of *Melencolia I*, as a reminder of scientific vanity. In an engraving attributed to the Master of 1515, a winged woman is interrupted from measuring an astrolobe by a man who points to a comet in the sky (fig. 11). Similarly, in an unattributed Venetian drawing of the early sixteenth century, a man distracts the attention of an astronomer by pointing to a luminary apparition, possibly a comet (fig. 12).[45] While the precise meaning of these graphic works cannot be adequately defined, it does seem clear that a contrast between earthly pursuits and the awareness of a higher order was intended. Also, the similarity to Brant's woodcut should not be neglected. Brant contrasts a measuring fool with a wise fool who indicates the futility of the former's labor by pointing to the words "Who measures heaven, earth, and sea, . . . Let him beware a fool to be." The full verse presumably follows. Furthermore, the contrast between the two fools corresponds to the contrasting states of awareness of Melancholy identified with her past and present. This does not imply that Dürer's Melancholy was intended to be interpreted on the same level as Brant's fool or the Italian astronomers. Rather, by conflating the two figures representing conflicting modes of knowledge, Dürer internalized the conflict thereby transforming Brant's geometer from

by Panofsky (*Dürer*, 71-72); see also Hoffmann, "Melencolia," 258, 262f.

[37] Ulrich Gaier, *Satire. Studien zu Neidhart, Wittenwiler, Brant und zur satirischen Schreibart* (Tübingen, 1967), 215-328, esp. 227f.; and Joël Lefebvre, *Les Fols et la Folie. Etude sur les genres du comique et la création littéraire en Allemagne pendant la Renaissance* (Paris, 1968).

[38] S. Brant, *The Ship of Fools*, trans. E. Zeydel (New York, 1944), 220. "Wer vsz misszt hymel, erd, vnd mer/ . . . Der lvg, das er dem narren wer"; see S. Brant, *Narrenschiff*, ed. F. Zarncke (Leipzig, 1854), 65.

[39] Brant, *Fools*, 220-221. Zeydel used the word *circle* to translate *zyrckel;* I have changed it to *compass* which is more accurate in this context. Brant, *Narrenschiff*, 65:
Ich halt den ouch nit jtel wisz
Der all syn synn leidt, vnd syn flisz
Wie er erkund all stett, vnd landt
Vnd nymbt den zyrckel jn die handt
Das er dar durch berichtet werd
Wie breit, wie lang, wie witt die erd
Wie dieff, vnd verr sich zieh das mer
Vnd was enthalt den letsten spor.

For the vanity of learning and mundane knowledge, see also chaps. 1, 27, 48.

[40] Brant, *Fools*, 224. "Was nott wont doch eym menschen by/ Das er such grössers dann er sy"; see Brant, *Narrenschiff*, 66.

[41] Brant, *Fools*, 222, 224; and *Narrenschiff*, 66:
Plinius der meyster seitt
Das es sy eyn vnsynnikeit
Wellen die grösz der welt verston
Vnd vsser der, byᵉwilen gon
Vnd rächnen bisz hynder das mer
Dar jnn menschlich vernunfft jrrt ser
Das sy solchem noch rächen allzyt
Vnd kan sich selb vsz rächen nitt, . . .
Vnd weiszt nit was jm nutz entspring
Wann er erfart schon hohe ding
Vnd nit die zyt syns todes kennt
Die wie eyn schätt von hynnan rennt.

[42] Augustine wrote that astronomers may be able to calculate when the sun will be eclipsed, but the false assurance of such knowledge can be grave: such men "by an impious pride, withdraw from Thee and forsake thy light. They foretell an eclipse of the sun before it happens, but they do not see their own eclipse which is even now occurring"; see *Confessions*, bk. 5, chap. 3 (trans. A. Outler [Philadelphia, 1955], 97). Agrippa relies on the same passage in Pliny (*Historia Naturalis*, *2:* i, 3) to arrive at a conclusion similar to Brant's; see Agrippa, *De Vanitate*, chap. 27.

[43] On vanity imagery in the engraving, see also M. Steck, "Theoretische Beiträge zu Albrecht Dürers Kupferstich 'Melencolia I' von 1514," *Forschungen und Fortschritte*, *32* (1958): 251; and Schuster, "Melencolia," 409-411.

[44] For the one exception, see Hoffmann, "Melencolia," 252f.

[45] Illus. in H. Tietze and E. Tietze-Conrat, *The Drawings of the Venetian Painters in the 15th and 16th Centuries* (New York, 1944), 134, A575; B. J. Meijer, "Early Drawings by Titian: some attribu-

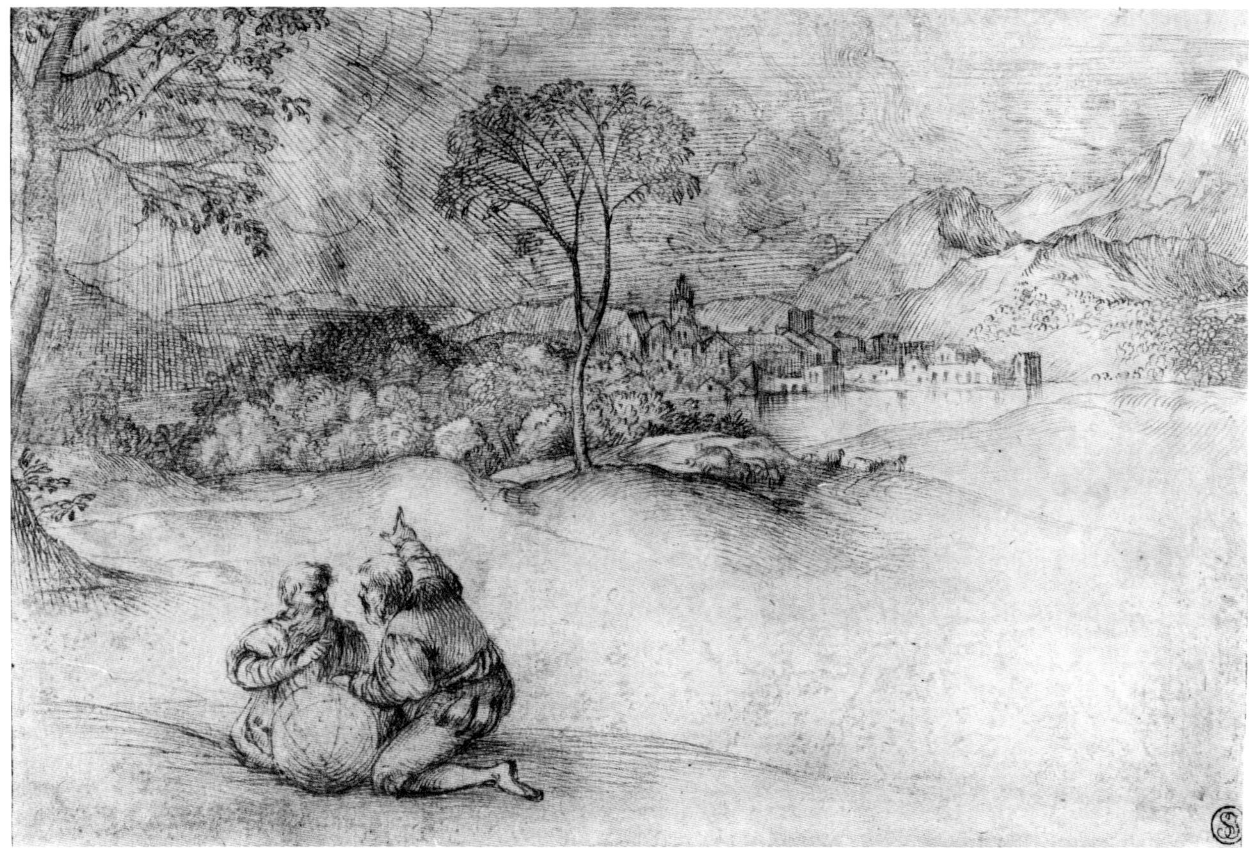

Fig. 12. Venetian school, Two Astronomers, *early 16th c. Pen and ink. Städelsches Kunstinstitut, Frankfurt*

tions," *Arte Veneta, 28* (1974): 88; D. Rosand and M. Muraro, *Titian and the Venetian Woodcut* (Washington, D.C., 1976), 201.

[46] Brant, *Narrenschiff,* 87-88:

Der furet vff eym strowen dach
Der vff der welt rum, setzt syn sach
Vnd all ding dut, vff zyttlich ere
Dem würt zu letst nüt anders me
Dan das syn won, jnn hatt betrogen
So er buwt vff eyn rägenbogen
We wölbet vff eyn dannyn sul
Dem würt ee zyt, syn anschlag ful.

For earlier expressions of this idea, see *Freidank,* ed. W. Grimm (Göttingen, 1860), 153:

Swer gote dienet âne wanc,
deist aller wîsheit anevanc.
swer umbe dise kurse zît
die êwigen fröude gît,
der hât sich selbe gar betrogen
und zimbert ûf den regenbogen;
swenne der regenboge zergât,
son weiz er wâ sîn hûs stât.

See also *Meister Altswert,* Bibliothek des Literarischen Vereins, 21, ed. A. Keller and W. Holland (Stuttgart, 1850), 161.

[47] The contributions of Aristotle and Albertus Magnus were summarized in the Renaissance by Gaetan

an embodiment of man's ceaseless folly into a compelling statement on the tragic limitations of man's mind.

While the comet serves primarily as a *memento mori,* the meaning of the rainbow is more complex. It both confirms Melancholy's geometric achievement of measuring the heavens and, simultaneously, acts as a reminder of her futile pursuit. Following an earlier literary tradition, Sebastian Brant used the rainbow as a metaphor of the vanity of men who are concerned only with the material world and earthly fame.[46] The rainbow was a particularly apt symbol to play this dual role of alluding to Melancholy's illusory success because, ever since Aristotle, the rainbow was recognized as nothing more than the reflection of the sun on a cloud, that is, an illusion itself.[47] Thus the rainbow, as an allusion to the celestial order, is nothing more than an illusion and reveals to Melancholy that her aspirations were built like a castle in the air.

The seemingly contradictory duality of the rainbow as a symbol accords perfectly with the earliest analysis of the engraving's symbolism, published in 1541 by Joachim Camerarius, Dürer's friend and director of the Protestant *Gymnasium* in Nuremberg. According to Camerarius, the ladder in *Melencolia I* symbolized both the aspiration toward heavenly or absolute truth, but at the same time the futility of that quest:

Next to her are seen the instruments of the arts, books, rulers, compasses, standards, even certain iron and wood works. But in order to indicate that nothing is usually comprehended by such talents and how these things are repeatedly reduced to absurdity, he raises up stairs before her into the clouds.[48]

The bat confirms Dürer's intention to include the theme of vanity within an iconographically ambivalent context. With "Melencolia I" emblazoned on its wings, the bat may be seen as one of the saturnine "daemons" which descend and provide inspiration,[49] an interpretation supported by the placement of the title on the wings suggesting the transitory nature of melancholic inspiration, or "winged inspiration." Yet the bat can also be understood as an embodiment of evil, indicated both by its demonic morphology and by its emblematic sources. The inscription on a late-fifteenth-century representation of *Frau Welt* identifies the bat with the sin of pride,[50] which is certainly applicable to Dürer's conception of the "geometer's melancholy" because, as Augustine, Cusa, Brant, and others recognized, the geometer's despair arose from his *proud* assumption that he could grasp the cosmos mathematically.[51] Horapollo specified the bat as a symbol of an unhealthy moral or mental condition causing incontinence.[52] Although the first edition of Horapollo was printed only in 1517, Dürer certainly was familiar with it before that date since he helped illustrate Pirckheimer's edition, presented to Emperor Maximilian in 1514.[53] Later literature also relied on the image of the bat's blind flight at night and specified the cause of the bat's morbidity. Alciati interpreted the bat as a symbol of folly in general, but more specifically as philosophical blindness which explores the universe by inappropriate means.[54] Camerarius cited the bat as a symbol of vain explorations and aspirations.[55] Although Alciati's and Camerarius' emblem books appeared after Dürer had finished his engraving, their ideas correspond so closely to the context of *Melencolia* that it may be conjectured that the artist was aware of an earlier, unrecorded tradition similar in content. The notions of sterile investigations and the intellectual myopia of godless pursuits are precisely those which are repeatedly stressed by Brant in Chapter 66. Dürer's bat is Brant's purblind fool metamorphosed.

This conclusion does not predicate that the alternate interpretation of the bat as the vehicle for saturnine inspiration should be dismissed as invalid. Like the rainbow and ladder, the bat embodied a meaningful iconographic duality. Indeed, most of the engraving's imagery is characterized by this apparent inconsistency.[56] On one level, the tools and instruments indicate the peculiar gifts of Melancholy, while on a secondary level the same objects are charged with religious significance.

If the engraving is interpreted as a temporal sequence, as I have suggested, then the two levels of meaning correspond to the past and present conditions of Melancholy. Within the realm of her geometrically inspired endeavors, the tools and instruments held no meaning for Melancholy beyond their prescribed, utilitarian function. Plunged into the "dense gloom" of reason,[57] Melancholy did not recognize the clues to God's presence which surrounded her, but with the appearance of the rainbow and comet, a higher sphere is revealed to her and her world is transformed.[58] The celestial light unveils the

de Thiene, *Meteorologicorum* (Venice, 1491); but see also: Gregor Reisch, *Margarita Philosphica* (Freiburg, 1503), bk. 9, chap. 22; Themo, *In quator libros meteororum*, ed. G. Lokert (Paris, 1518), 177-204. Although the existence of lunar rainbows were denied by Pliny (*Historie of the World* [London, 1601], 28, II, LX), they were accepted as reality during the Renaissance: Aristotle, *Meteorologica*, ed. G. da Thiene (Venice, 1522), 372.

[48] Joachim Camerarius, *Elementa rhetoricae* (Basel, 1541), 138-139; quoted in Rupprich, *Nachlass, 1:* 319: "Ut autem indicaret, nihil non talibus ab ingeniis comprehendi solere, et quam eadem saepenumero in absurda defferrentur, ante illam scalas in nubes eduxit, per quarum gradus quadratum saxum veluti ascensionem moliri fecit." I am indebted to Robert Newman for his help with this passage. It was quoted by Wrampelmeyer (*Ungedruckte Schriften Philipp Melanchthons*, Beilage zum Jahresberichte des Kgl. Gymnasiums zu Clausthal [1911], 8, n. 62) and by Klibansky et al. (*Saturn*, 320, n. 121) as by Melanchthon.

[49] Horst, "Melencolia I," 417-419; Klibansky et al., *Saturn*, 320-323.

[50] Hoffmann, "Melencolia," 252: "Sertum pavonis, alas vespertilionis mundus habet stultus prebet calicem babilonis Corde lupi sordet ut draco sibi mordet."

[51] Augustine, *Confessions*, bk. 5, chap. 3; Cusa, *De Visione Dei, 9:* 103; Brant, *Narrenschiff;* Adriano Castellesi, *De vera philosophia* (Cologne, 1540), *3:* chaps. 12-13, fols. I6r-K5v. As a confirmation of Melancholy's pride, Dürer might have intended the dog (W. Hempel, *Übermuot Diu Alte . . . Der Superbia-Gedanke* [Bonn, 1970], 205) and the tower (Hoffmann, "Melencolia," 262-264) as symbols of pride.

[52] *Hori Apollinis Niliaci Hieroglyphica hoc est de sacri Aegyptiorum literis Libelli duo de Graeco i Latinum sermo nem a Philippo Phasianino Bononiensi nunc primum translati* (1517), fol. 30r (bk. 2, chap. 51); cited by Klibansky et al., *Saturn*, 323.

[53] K. Giehlow, "Die Hieroglyphenkunde des Humanismus in der Allegorie der Renaissance," *Jahrbuch des Kunsthistorischen Sammlungen des Allerhöchsten Kaiserhauses, 32* (1915): 170f.

[54] Andrea Alciati, *Emblemata* (Rovilium, 1551), 69-70:

Vespertilio
Assumpsisse suum volucri ex Meneide nomen,
Socraticum auctores Choerephoonta ferunt.
Fusca viro facies, & stridens vocula, tali
Hunc hominem potuit commaculare nota.

* * * * * *

Vespere quae tantum volitat, qvae lumine lusca est,
Quae cum alas gestet, caetera muris habet:
Adres diversae trahitur mala nomina primvm
Signat: quae latitant, iudiciumque timent.
Inde & philosophos, qui dum caelestia quaerunt,
Caligant oculis, falsaque sola vident.
Tandem & versutos, cum clam sectentur vtrumque,
Acquirunt neutra qui sibi parte fidem.

Cited by Rossmann, "Wert und Grenze," 136ff; and Günter Bandmann, *Melancholie und Musik* (Cologne, 1960), 88. For a similar passage, see E. Schön's woodcut of *Clean and Unclean Animals*, c.1534, in which the bat is described:

true nature of the saturnine bat, which flies in fear of the light, and simultaneously the light discloses the means of salvation through Christ. Thus the duality of the engraving's symbols can be seen as an eloquent symbol itself, expressive of Melancholy's profound Christian revelation. By planning disparate ideas within each object, Dürer has created a *coincidentia oppositorum* which conveys the transfigured vision of an enlightened Melancholy.

AUTHOR'S NOTE

The astute criticism of Professors Egon Verheyen, Konrad Hoffman, and Craig Harbison has clarified many of my ideas concerning Dürer's famous *Vexierbild*.

"Die Fledermaus fleugt bey der nacht
Also der gotlosz wirdt geacht
Der sein werck haimlich tückisch thut
Wann sie seind unreht und nit gut."

(illus. in Geisberg, *Woodcut, 1:* 1139.)

[55]J. Camerarius, *Symbolorvm et Emblematvm* (1596), n. 89; cited by Bandmann, *Melancholie,* 88.

[56]The concept of *coincidorum oppositorum* was popular in philosophy and literature, but its application in the arts has been generally discounted. Recently, S. Adams ("The Anterotica of Petrus Haedus: A Fifteenth-century Model for the Interpretation of Symbolic Images," *Renaissance and Reformation, 14* [1978]: 111-126) has elucidated a late-fifteenth-century text which establishes the possibility of coinciding but divergent meanings within a single picture.

[57]J. Colet, *Enarratio in Epistolam S. Pauli ad Romanos,* ed. and trans. J. J. Lupton (London, 1873), 163. The metaphor was so extensively used during the sixteenth century that even a summary would require a lengthy article. It is interesting to note that the image of the twilight world of reason was particularly popular with Luther; see for example Luther, *Werke* (Weimer, 1883), *1:* 36 (Sermon on the feast day of St. Stephan, 1515) and 148; *10* (1910): pt. 1, p. 181f. (Christmas sermon of 1522); *56* (1938): 355.

[58]J. P. Migne, *Patrologiae Latina, 76:* 868. St. Gregory described the effects of the rainbow as intended "to recall the hearts of believers": "Qui arcus in nabe est in die pluviae, quia in dominica incarnatione, et in effusione praedicationis ostend tur, ut ad veniam corda credentium, e Domino parcente, revocentur."

The Portrait of Sir Brian Tuke by Hans Holbein the Younger

JOHN OLIVER HAND

In late August of the year 1526 Hans Holbein the Younger left the city of Basel for England, traveling by way of the Rhine Valley to the Netherlands. He carried with him letters of introduction from that prince of humanists Erasmus of Rotterdam, who was then residing in Basel and whose portrait Holbein had painted in 1523.[1] In a letter to Peter Aegidius, town clerk of Antwerp, Erasmus explained Holbein's reasons for leaving the Swiss city: "The arts are freezing in this part of the world, and he is on his way to England to pick up some angels there."[2]

Holbein's first sojourn in England lasted from 1526 to 1528 and was both a financial and an artistic success. Thanks to Erasmus' introduction Holbein was able to meet Sir Thomas More and spend a good deal of time with him. During this period More was renowned as a brilliant and learned humanist, as the author of *Utopia*, and as parliamentarian and member of the court of Henry VIII. Holbein's association with More was advantageous in that it put the artist in touch with the circle of literati who enjoyed the great scholar's friendship. Like More, however, many of these people also worked for King Henry VIII, who had gathered around him men who were both able administrators and scholars. Many of Holbein's portrait commissions came from this group, and, of course, the best-known image of Sir Thomas More is Holbein's portrait of 1527 in the Frick Collection, New York (fig. 1).[3] While the portrait of More has been studied in extenso, Holbein's portrait of Sir Brian Tuke in the National Gallery of Art has not received the critical examination it deserves. This study is an attempt to rectify that situation.

Sir Brian Tuke (fig. 2) is shown in half-length against a mottled greenish-brown background.[4] He wears a soft black cap with ear flaps and a black cape with brown fur collar and meticulously

[1] Several portraits of Erasmus exist: a painting in the collection of the earl of Radnor, Longford Castle, Salisbury, is dated 1523; portraits in the Offentliche Kunstsammlung, Basel, and the Musée du Louvre, Paris, have been dated to 1523 and 1523/24 respectively. See P. Ganz, *The Paintings of Hans Holbein* (London, 1950), cat. nos. 34-36, pls. 64-66.

[2] A. B. Chamberlain, *Hans Holbein the Younger* (New York, 1913), *1:* 255.

[3] Chamberlain, *Holbein, 1:* 303-304; Ganz, *Holbein,* cat. no. 41; S. Morison, *The Likeness of Thomas More* (New York, 1963), 7-10; see also the catalogue by J. B. Trapp and H. S. Herbrüggen that accompanied the exhibition *'The King's Good Servant' Sir Thomas More 1477/8-1535* at the National Portrait Gallery, London, Nov. 25, 1977–Mar. 12, 1978.

[4] National Gallery of Art no. 65, Andrew W. Mellon Collection, 1937. Wood, 49 x 39 cm (19⅜ x 15¼ in). Provenance: Sir Paul Methuen (1672-1757), Corsham Court, Wiltshire; Paul Cobb Methuen, Wiltshire; Paul, First Lord Methuen of Corsham, Wiltshire (probably sold after 1838); Richard Sanderson, Edinburgh (sold 1848); Richard, second marquess of Westminster; Lady Theodora Guest, Inwood, Somersetshire; (M. Knoedler & Co., New York, 1913) Watson B. Dickermann, New York (between 1914 and 1929); (M. Knoedler & Co., New York) Andrew W. Mellon, Pittsburgh (by 1930); National Gallery of Art, 1937.

Exhibitions: London, South Kensington Museum, *The Third National Portrait Exhibition,* 1868, no. 625; London, Royal Academy, *Old Masters,* 1880, no. 188; London, Burlington Fine Arts Club, *Early English Portraiture,* 1909, no. 43; New York, Knoedler Galleries, *Masterpieces of Old and Modern Painters,* 1915, no. 4.

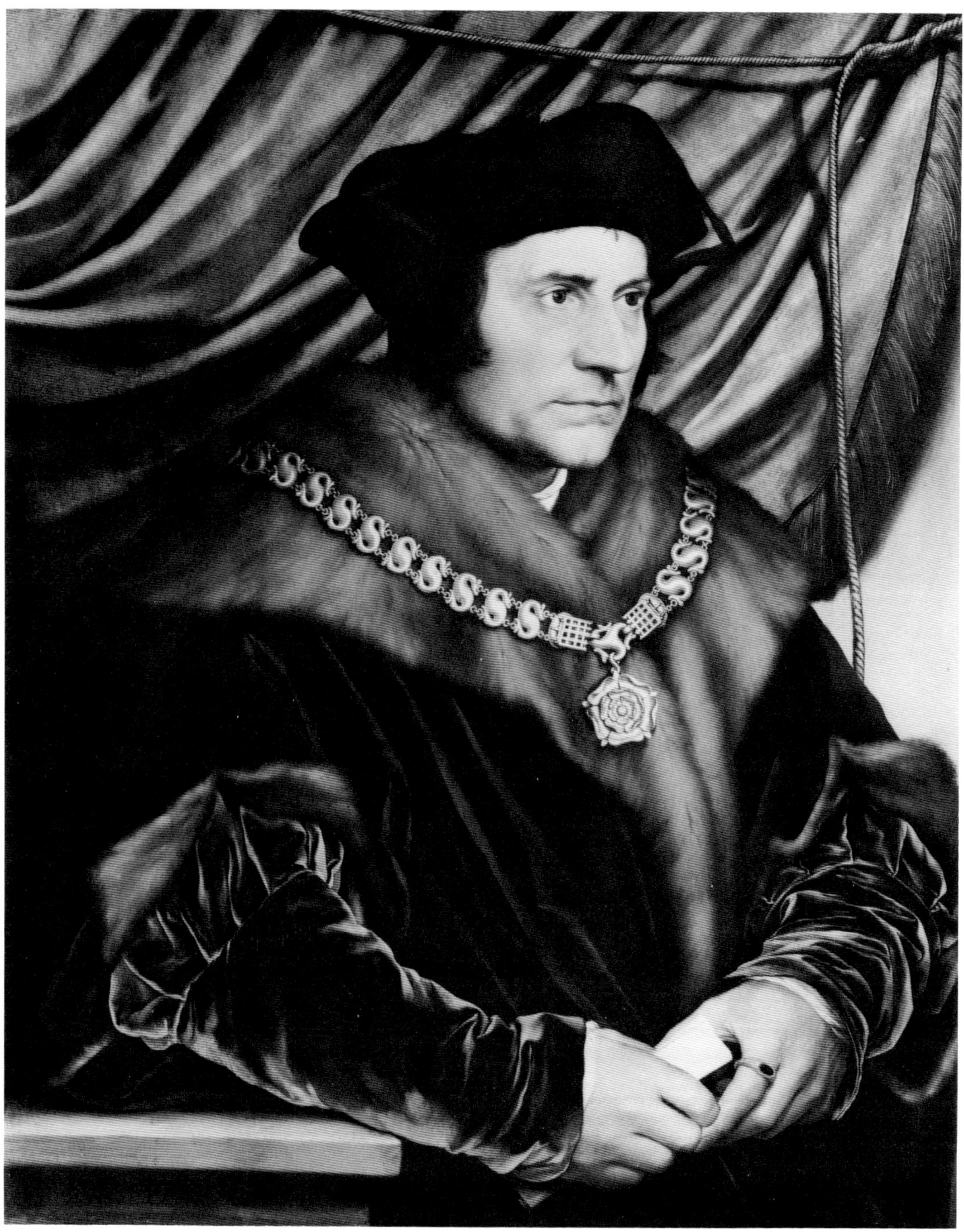

Fig. 1. Hans Holbein the Younger, Sir Thomas More, *1527. Wood. Copyright, The Frick Collection, New York*

rendered cloth-of-gold sleeves. A pair of gloves held in the left hand and a crucifix suspended from a heavy gold chain complete the costume. In the foreground is a folded piece of paper bearing a Latin inscription from the Book of Job. The sitter is identified at the top of the panel: BRIANVS TVKE, MILES, AN ETATIS SVAE LVII. Below this is Tuke's personal motto DROIT ET AVANT ("upright and forward").[5]

[5] Infra-red and ultra-violet photography as well as first-hand examination of the painting do not confirm the assertion of Ganz, *Holbein*, 234, cat. no. 51, that the topmost inscription and the quotation from Job are later additions. We can assume they are contemporary with the rest of the painting. Interestingly, the motto DROIT ET AVANT is also to be found on a retable of the Passion, carved in Brussels

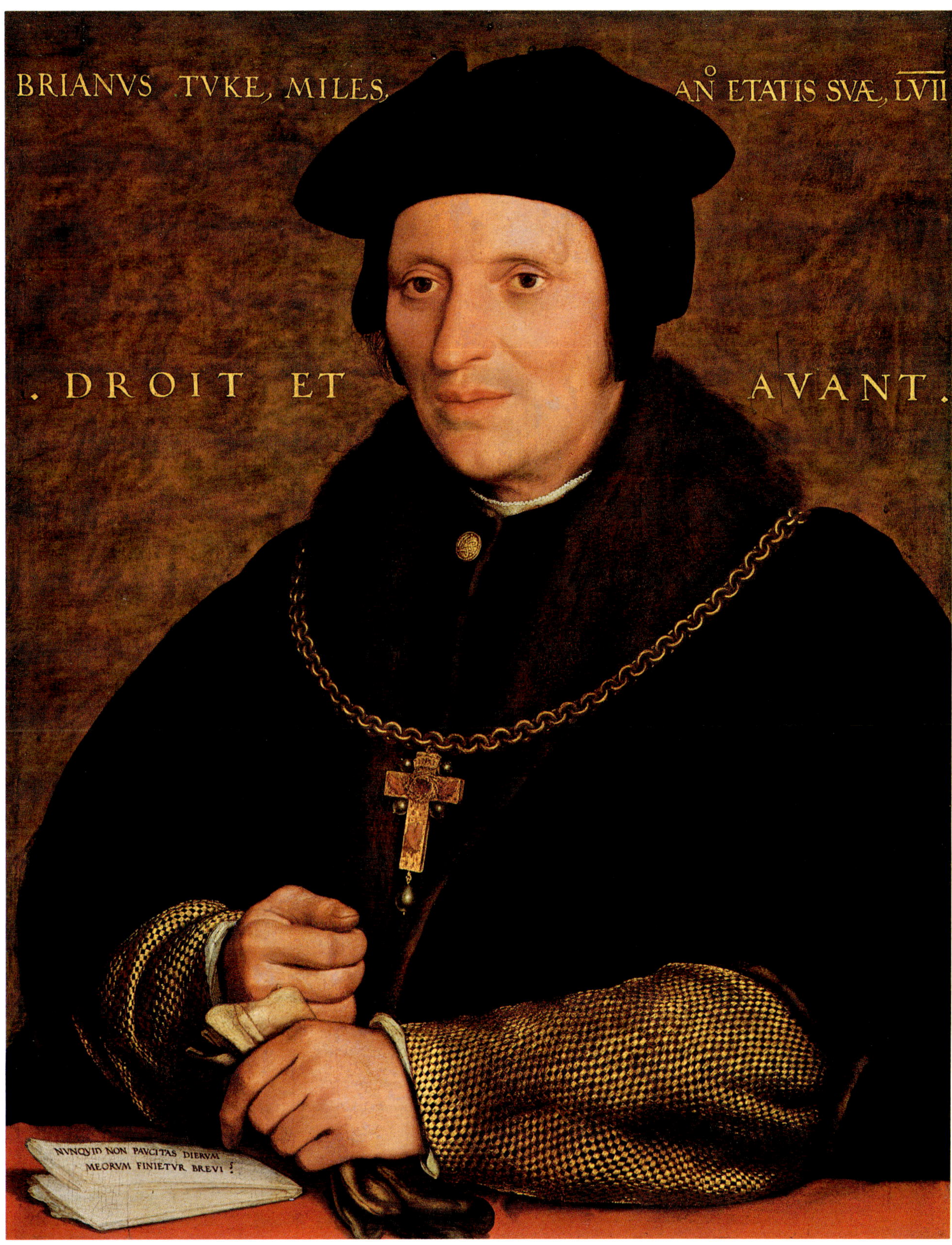

Fig. 2. Hans Holbein the Younger, Sir Brian Tuke, *1528 or 1532/33. Wood. National Gallery of Art, Washington, D.C.; Andrew W. Mellon Collection, 1937*

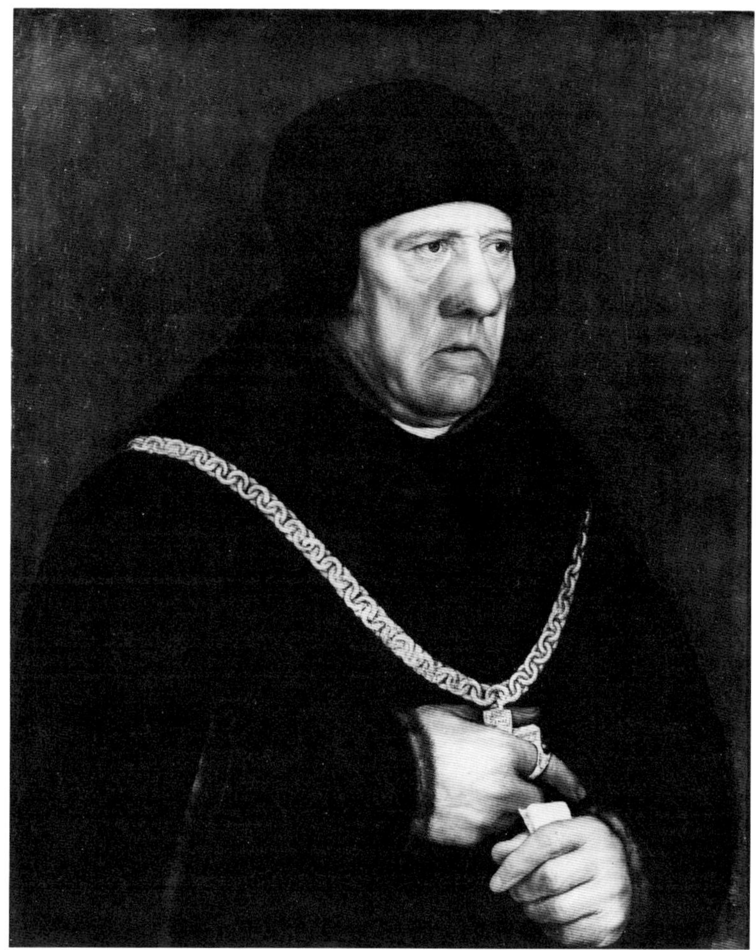

Fig. 3. Hans Holbein the Younger, Sir Henry Wyatt, *1527/28. Wood. Musée du Louvre, Paris. Photo: Cliché des Musées Nationaux, Paris*

Although the panel is not signed, the attribution to Holbein is almost universally accepted. However, the year of Brian Tuke's birth is not known and so the date of the picture cannot be established from the sitter's age. Most scholars agree in dating the portrait to Holbein's first English period, 1526-1528; a few critics, however, believe the date should be pushed up to 1532/33, the beginning of the second English period, and a date as late as 1540/41 has also been proposed.[6] On stylistic grounds alone there is much to recommend a date in the first English period; one has only to compare the portrait of Tuke with such works as the Sir Thomas More of 1527 or the Sir Henry Wyatt (fig. 3) of 1527/28 in the Louvre.[7]

In addition, if we accept provisionally that the National Gallery's portrait was painted in 1528 when he was fifty-seven years old, then he would have been born around 1471. He was probably the son of Richard and Agnes Tuke.[8] Richard was said to have been tutor to the Duke of Norfolk, and it is possibly because of this connection with the Duke of Norfolk that Brian Tuke obtained his first public position in 1508, that of king's bailiff in Sandwich. Other positions followed rapidly; in 1509 he was clerk of the signet and also was

around 1470 for Claudio Villa and Gentina Solaro and now in the Musées Royaux d'Art et d'Histoire, Brussels. See G. Derveaux-van Ussel, *Retables en Bois,* Musées Royaux d'Art et d'Histoire (Brussels, 1977), 9, pl. 5. It is not known when Tuke first used this motto or from where he derived it.

[6] Chamberlain, *Holbein, 1:* 331, gives a date of 1527 or 1528; W. Stein, *Holbein* (Berlin, 1929), 159, dates the portrait to the end of the first English period; C. L. Kuhn, *A Catalogue of German Paintings of the Middle Ages and Renaissance in American Collections* (Cambridge, Mass., 1936), 79-80, cat. no. 351, says "about 1526-1528"; Ganz, *Holbein,* 234, cat. no. 51, proposes either 1528 or 1532/33; H. A. Schmid, *Hans Holbein der Jungere. Sein Aufstieg zur Meisterschaft und sein Englischer Stil* (Basel, 1948), *2:*282, 386, suggests the period 1532-1536; L. Cust, "A Portrait of Queen Catherine Howard, by Hans Holbein the Younger," *The Burlington Magazine, 17* (1910): 194, puts forward, without explanation, a date of 1540-1541; R. Salvini and H. W. Grohn, *L'Opera pittorica completa di Holbein il Giovane* (Milan, 1971), cat. no. 120, also date the panel to 1539-1541.

appointed feodary, an officer authorized to collect rents, for Wallingford and St. Walric. In October of 1510 he was made clerk of the Council of Calais and served on the commission of the peace for Kent in 1512 and for Essex in 1513, presumably as a clerk.

In 1516 Brian Tuke was made a "Knight of the King's Body" and in the following year was named "Governor of the King's Posts," a position of power and responsibility that he kept throughout his career. As the equivalent of our postmaster general, Tuke was charged with ensuring that domestic letters were delivered promptly and safely; also he seems to have been responsible for arranging payment for messengers and couriers operating on the king's business in Europe.

Sometime after 1517 Sir Brian Tuke became secretary to Cardinal Wolsey, and in 1522 he attained the position of French secretary to King Henry VIII. In April of the following year he was granted clerkship of Parliament. Tuke's abilities must have impressed Henry, for in 1528 he was one of the commissioners appointed to treat for peace with France and, perhaps more importantly, was made treasurer of the royal household. Tuke held a position of considerable responsibility, and a very great number of the surviving documents either refer to or are addressed to Sir Brian Tuke. In addition to his duties as postmaster, treasurer, and French secretary, he was also in demand as a skilled cryptographer who could deciper communiqués from the Continent.[9] During this period Tuke was also a member of the circle of savants gathered around Sir Thomas More, and he apparently was regarded as a speaker and writer of great eloquence.[10]

The 1530s saw a change in both the climate and the personalities at the court of Henry VIII. Cardinal Wolsey died in 1530; Archbishop Wareham died in 1532; Sir Thomas More was sent to the Tower of London in 1534 and beheaded the following year. The liberal humanism of the 1520s gave way to the religious and social storms that accompanied Henry's divorce and his struggle to establish the supremacy of the crown over the Church. Tuke not only weathered the crises, he prospered. He wrote the preface to the edition of *The Workes of Geffray Chaucer* by William Thynne published in 1532, and in 1533 he served as sheriff of Essex and Hertfordshire.[11] Tuke was by now a seasoned professional, and his mastery of the survival skills of the civil servant can be seen in his reply of August 17, 1533, to Thomas Cromwell's charges of "grete defaulte in conveyance of letters."[12] Tuke adoitly shifts attention to the circumstances that do not allow him enough money for horses and riders and cites those people who "have dated their letters a day or 2 bifore they wer writen, and the conveyers have had the blame." Sir Brian Tuke died on October 26, 1545, at Layer Marney, one of several manors in Essex presented to him by the king. He was buried next to his wife Grissel, who had died in 1538, in St. Margaret's Lothbury.

Given Tuke's position and importance it is not surprising to find that Holbein's original picture in the National Gallery of Art was copied several times. A portrait of Brian Tuke is mentioned in John Evelyn's *Diary* for August 27, 1678, as belonging to Lord Lisle, but it has not been successfully associated with any extant work.[13] In addition to at least three versions mentioned in the literature of the

[7] Reproduced in Ganz, *Holbein,* pl. 87.

[8] The biography of Brian Tuke that follows is based primarily on the information found in the *Dictionary of National Biography* (London, 1937), *19:* 1222-1223. See also J. Piggot, "Sir Brian Tuke," *The Athenaeum,* Sept. 25, 1869, 408-409.

[9] Tuke's name appears literally hundreds of times in J. S. Brewer, ed., *Letters and Papers, Foreign and Domestic, of the Reign of Henry VIII* (London, 1862 et. seq.). For one example of Tuke's reputation as a cryptographer see the above, *4,* pt. 1, no. 4103, Mar. 27, 1528, in which Gardiner and Foxe writing from Orvieto request Tuke "to take some trouble in deciphering their ciphers, as they know his skill."

[10] Tuke's fame can be inferred from the lavish praise given him by his contemporary, the famous antiquarian John Leland (c. 1506-1552) in: *Principum, Ac illustrium aliquot & eruditorium in Anglia virorum, Encomia, Trophaea, Genethliaca, & Epithalamia* (London, 1589), 4, 15-16, 22-23, 31, 34, 38, 41, 47-48, 77. These verses and epigrams, not published until after Leland's death, were originally presented to Henry VIII.

[11] The full title is *The Workes of Geffray Chaucer Newly Printed, with Dyvers Which Were Never in Print Before* (London, Thomas Godfray, 1532). Thynne's edition is especially important because it is the first collection of Chaucer's works with any claim to completeness. The preface is dedicated to Henry VIII and appears to be by Thynne; however, Tuke's authorship is confirmed by the inscription in a copy of the book at Clare College, Cambridge, which reads, "This preface I Sir Brian Tuke knight wrot at the request of Mr. Clarke of the kechyn then being tarying for the tyde at Grenewich"; quoted in the *Dictionary of National Biography* (London, 1898) *56:* 374. I am indebted to R. D. Gooder, fellows' librarian at Clare College, for sending me a photocopy of the preface showing the inscription in Tuke's vigorous hand. See also E. P. Hammand, *Chaucer, A Bibliographical Manual* (New York, 1933), 116.

[12] Tuke's letter is quoted in full in *State Papers Published under the Authority of His Majesty's Commission* (London, 1830). 404-406.

[13] E. S. de Beer, ed., *The Diary of John Evelyn* (Oxford, 1955) *4:* 142-143.

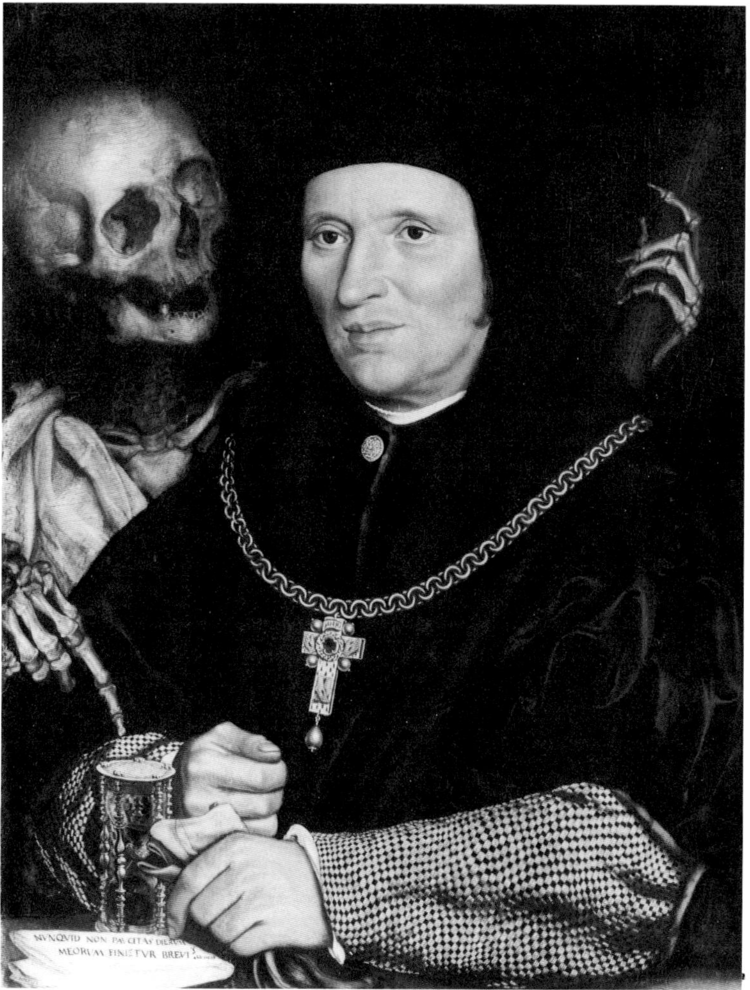

Fig. 4. After Hans Holbein the Younger, Sir Brian Tuke, *Wood. Bayerischen Staatsgemäldesammlungen, Munich*

nineteenth century,[14] there exist copies, in the Alte Pinakothek, Munich (fig. 4); the Norton Simon Museum of Art, Pasadena (fig. 5); and only recently come to light, the Art Market, Germany (fig. 6).[15] Interestingly, the only images of Tuke that survive follow the Holbein model.

Thus far, we have considered only the public image, the official career of Sir Brian Tuke. Holbein's portrait also sheds light on the private, emotional life of the sitter. A major clue to the meaning of this picture is provided by the words on the folded paper in the foreground to which Tuke seems to be pointing with the finger of his left hand (fig. 7). The inscription *Nvnqvid non Pavcitas Diervm Meorvm Finietvr Brevi?* from the Book of Job (10:20) as found in the Latin Vulgate, may be translated, "Shall not my few days be ended shortly?" These are the words spoken by Job in the midst of his afflictions and his expostulations to God.

The Book of Job is one of the most magnificent works of literature and theology in the Old Testament; its uniqueness caused Luther to state, "I look upon the book of Job as a true history, yet I do not

[14] T. H. D. writing in *The Athenaeum,* Sept. 13, 1869, 376, cites a painting on canvas in the possession of William M. Tuke, Saffron, Walden, and one in the collection of the late Reverend Nicholas Tuke, Godington, Kent, in 1864. A third portrait of Tuke is listed as being in the collection of J. R. Haig in *Notes and Queries,* 4th ser., 5 (Mar. 26, 1870): 313. The present location of these paintings is unknown.

[15] Bayerischen Staatsgemäldesammlungen, Munich; inv. no. 737, oak, 49 x 38 cm (19¼ x 15 in). The Norton Simon Foundation, Los Angeles; inv. no. F.651.30.P, wood, 49.5 x 38.5 cm (19½ x 15⅛ in). Dr. A. Deér, Atelier Helvetica, Konstanz; oak, 49 x 38.5 cm (19¼ x 15⅛ in).

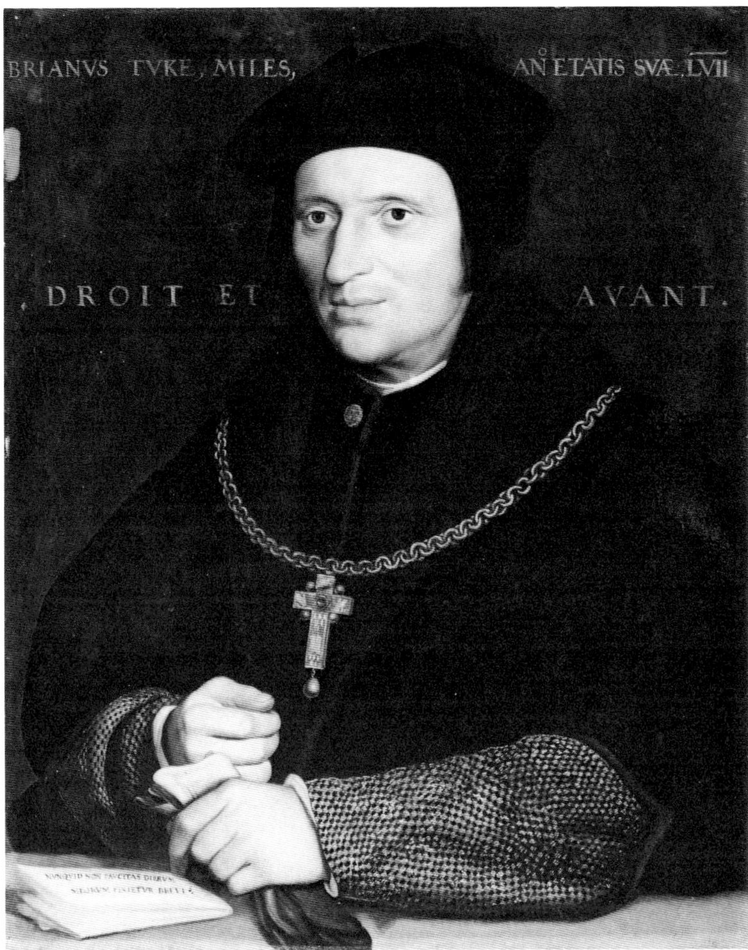

Fig. 5. After Hans Holbein the Younger, Sir Brian Tuke, *Wood. The Norton Simon Foundation, Los Angeles*

believe that all took place just as it is written, but that an ingenious, pious and learned man brought it into its present form."[16] The Book of Job addresses the sufferings of the just and such questions as whether goodness can exist without reward, or whether man in the midst of misfortune can understand the wisdom and plans of God. Throughout the Middle Ages and the Renaissance the figure of Job is viewed both as an exemplar of patience, of perseverant faith, and as a prophet of the resurrection of Christ—this last-named function is based on the famous passage (19:25-26), "For I know that my Redeemer lives, and at last he will stand upon the earth; and after my skin has been thus destroyed, then from my flesh I shall see God, . . ."

I would suggest that Job, who suffers undeserved and incomprehensible afflictions, would have had special significance and poignant relevance for man in the early sixteenth century whose own faith and understanding was being severely tested. We find quotations from the Book of Job used on portraits as personal mottos and momentoes. One example of this can be seen in the National Gallery's *Portrait of a Lady* attributed to Ludger tom Ring the Elder of 1532 (fig. 10).[17] There is certainly a deliberate contrast intended between the woman's prosperous, fashionable attire and the inscrip-

[16] W. Smith, *Smith's Bible Dictionary* (New York, 1967), 303.

[17] National Gallery of Art no. 700, wood, 44.5 x 32 cm (17½ x 12½ in), gift of Chester Dale, 1942.

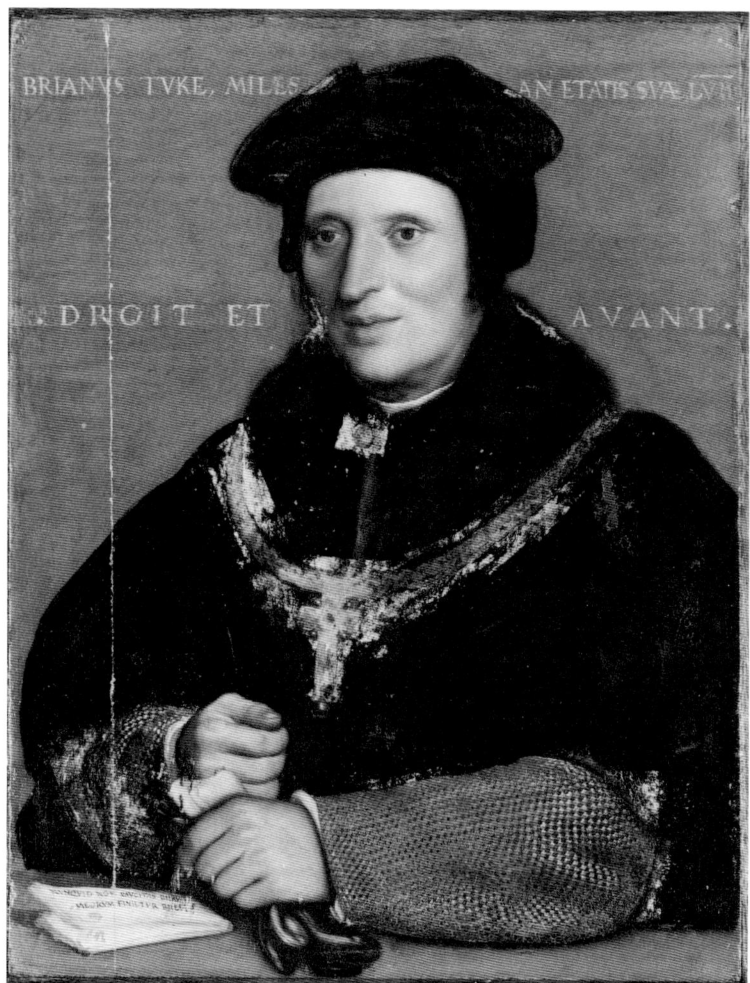

Fig. 6. After Hans Holbein the Younger, Sir Brian Tuke, *Wood. Art Market, Germany. (Shown stripped of old repaint)*

tion from Job (1:21) at the top of the panel, *Bloes bin ich auss muther Leib kome. Bloes werd ich wider hin gan.* ("Naked came I out of my mother's womb and naked shall I return thither"). It is interesting and, I believe, indicative of Job's position in early sixteenth-century thought that both this anonymous woman and Brian Tuke went to the Book of Job for the kind of language that would express their awareness of the incertitude of life, the impermanence of worldly possessions, or the nearness of death.

The relationship between Job and Christ has been examined in detail by Professor Gert von der Osten.[18] He has established a typological and visual interchange between Job seated on the dung-heap (or ash-heap in the Hebrew version) and a variation on the devotional image of the Man of Sorrows known as "Christ in Distress" *(Christ im Elend).* This connection can be seen in a comparison of the figure of Job on the dung-heap on one wing of Albrecht Dürer's Jabach altar of 1502-1504 (fig. 8)[19] with Holbein's drawing from 1519 of *Christ Seated on the Cross (Christ in Distress)* (fig. 9) in the Kupferstichkabinett, Berlin.[20] It is not necessary to assume that

[18] G. von der Osten, "Job and Christ," *Journal of the Warburg and Courtauld Institutes,* 16 (1953): 153-158.

[19] For discussion and earlier literature, see F. Anzelewsky, *Albrecht Dürer, Das Malerische Werk* (Berlin, 1971), 175-179.

[20] P. Ganz, *Handzeichnungen Hans Holbein des Jüngern in Auswahl* (Basel, 1943), pl. 4, p. 31. Inv. no. KdZ 14729; pen and ink on brown toned paper, washed with brush and watercolor, white heightening, 16.0 x 20.5 cm ($6^{5}/_{16}$ x $8^{1}/_{16}$ in). The Dürer monogram is a later addition.

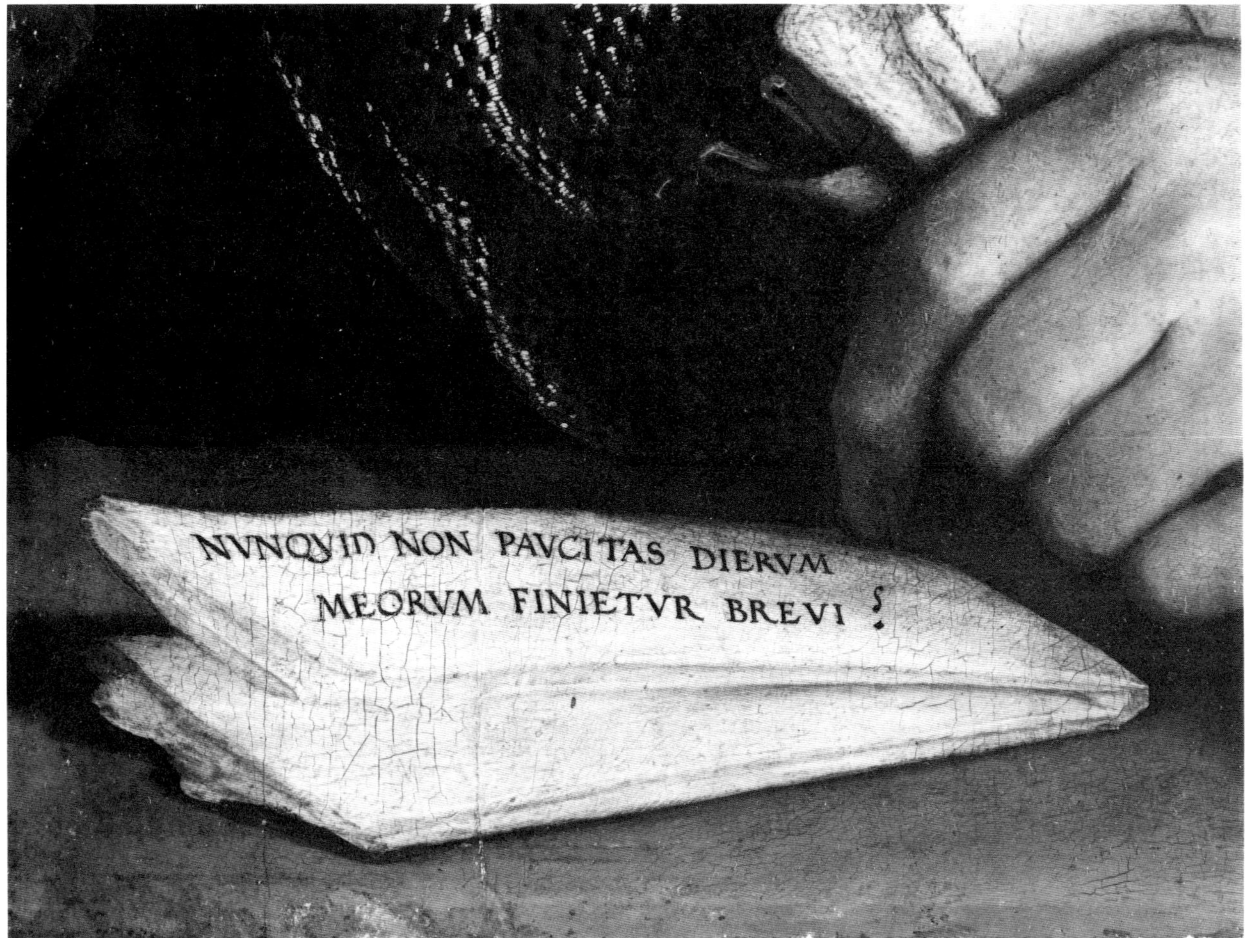

Fig. 7. Hans Holbein the Younger, Sir Brian Tuke *(detail of fig. 2)*

Holbein knew Dürer's altar, although that is possible; rather the pose of Holbein's Christ and Dürer's Job are both derived from traditional representations of Job in medieval manuscripts and sculpture. The typological association of Job with Christ, of suffering, death, and resurrection leads us to a consideration of the most intriguing object in Holbein's portrait, the crucifix worn by Sir Brian Tuke.

The cross (fig. 11) is almost certainly made of gold, and at its center is a red gem stone, probably a ruby, which signifies the wound in the Lord's heart and which is encircled by the Crown of Thorns. At the extremities, apparently rendered in flesh-colored enamel, are the hands and feet of the crucified Christ. Additionally, the top of the cross bears the letters INRI (for *Iesus Nazarenus, Rex Iudaeorum*—"Jesus of Nazareth, King of the Jews") and is decorated with five black pearls.

This crucifix with its representation of the Five Wounds of Christ is quite possibly unique, for after several years of searching I have found no comparable examples. Similarly, it has not been possible to fix the date and country of origin with any precision, although several specialists have suggested that the cross is English and dates from the early sixteenth century.[21]

While the Gospels mention only the piercing of the Lord's side at

[21] A. G. Somers Cocks, Department of Metalwork, Victoria and Albert Museum, London, has stated in correspondence that the crucifix is possibly English and dates from the early sixteenth century; concurring in this opinion is John Cherry, Department of Medieval and Later Antiquities, British Museum, London. John Hayward and Charles Oman, in a joint opinion, see no reason why the cross should not be English or the work of a goldsmith resident in England. Priscilla Muller, Hispanic Society of America, New York, doubts that the crucifix is of Hispanic origin. There are a few extant crucifixes that, while not identical, might be generally compared to the Tuke cross: the reliquary cross of the early sixteenth century found at Downside Abbey, near Bath, England (see *The Antiquaries Journal,* 17 [1937]: 200-202; I am indebted to John Cherry for bringing this cross to my attention); an early seventeenth-century cross in the collection of the Hispanic Society of America, reproduced in P. Muller, *Jewels in Spain 1500-1800* (New York, 1972), fig. 72. Muller, *Jewels,* 50, mentions a jewel in the possession of Juana la Loca which had on its reverse a representation of the Five Wounds. Holbein was himself an accomplished designer of jewelry and goldsmith's work, but there is no reason to assume that he had a hand in the creation of Tuke's crucifix.

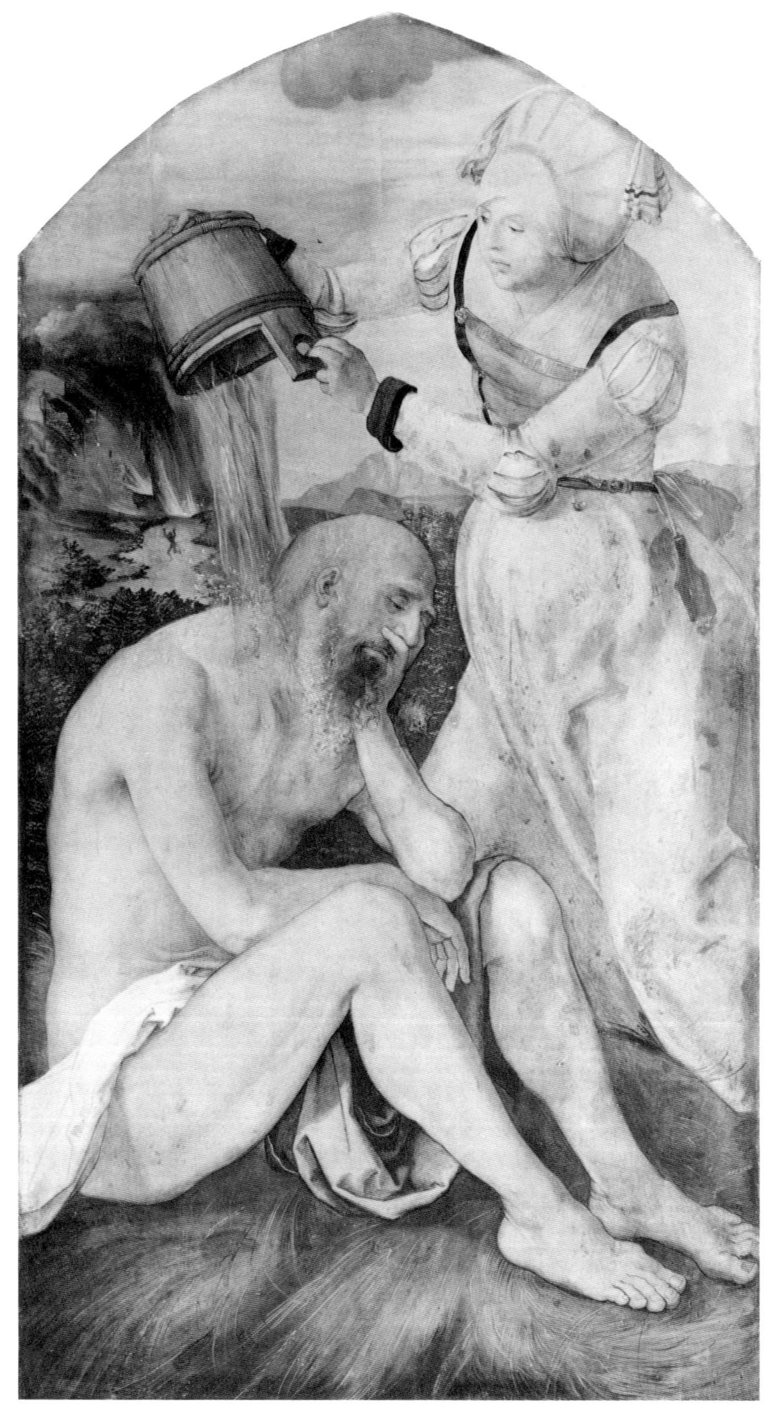

Fig. 8. Albrecht Dürer, Job and his Wife, *1502-1504. Wood. Städelsches Kunstinstitut, Frankfurt am Main*

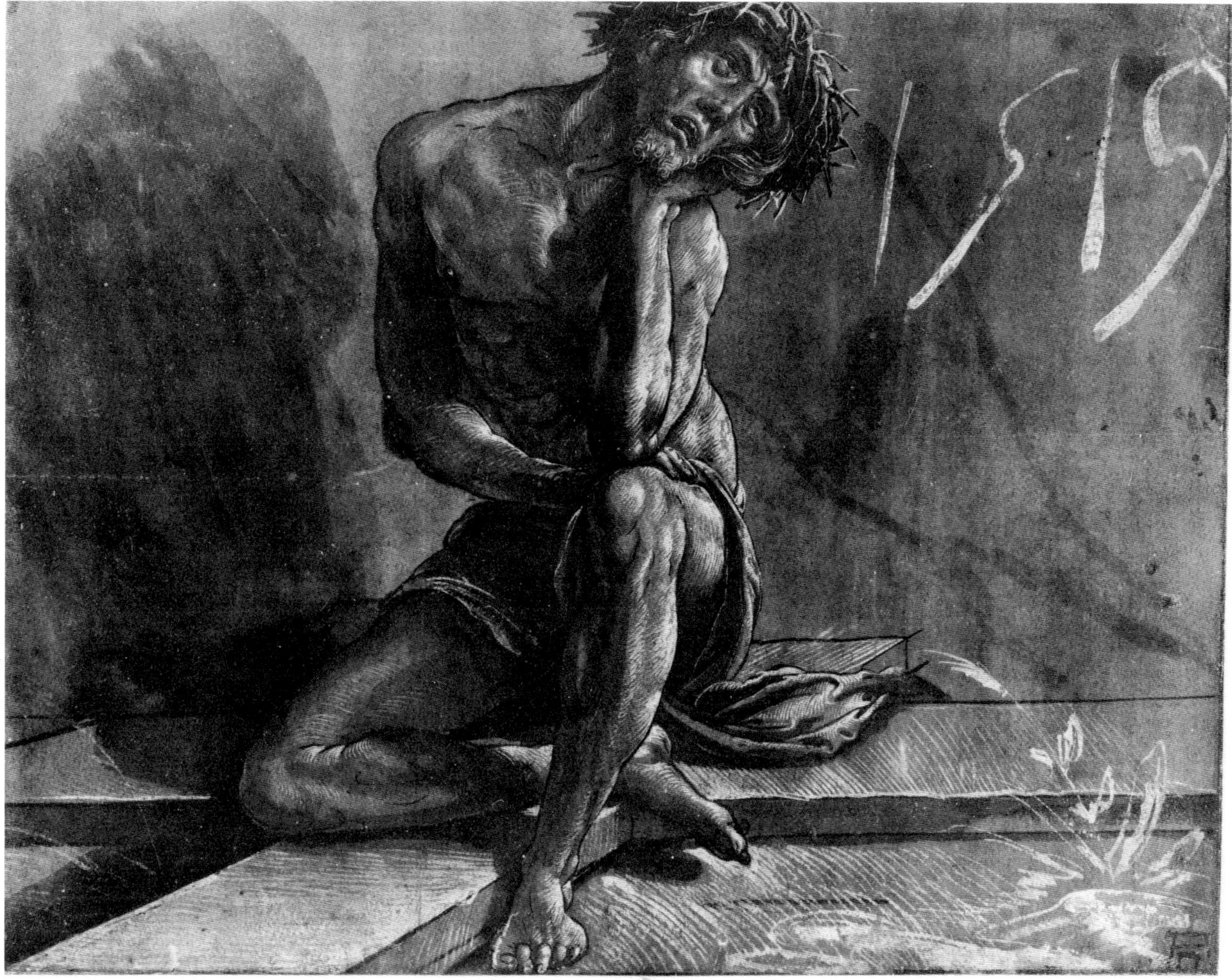

Fig. 9. Hans Holbein the Younger, Christ Seated on the Cross (Christ in Distress), *1519. Pen and ink and brush and watercolors, heightened with white, on toned paper. Staatliche Museen, Preussischer Kulturbesitz Kupferstichkabinett, Berlin*

the time of the crucifixion, accounts by Luke (24:39) and John (20:20) of the appearance of Christ after the Resurrection mention that the feet and hands were also pierced. In general, the theological significance of the Five Wounds is the same as that of the Crucifixion itself: the ultimate sacrifice undergone by Christ to redeem sinful mankind. It was not, however, until the later Middle Ages that it became an object of independent veneration; the cult of and devotion to the Five Wounds of Christ is essentially a product of the affective piety of the twelfth and thirteenth centuries.[22] One of the theologians most responsible for promoting the new devotion was St. Bernard of Clairvaux (1090-1153), who, for example, asks that in meditating on the Passion of Christ we "suffer so intensely with him that we shall ourselves be redeemed."[23] Equally influential were the teachings of St. Francis of Assisi (1182-1226), who advocated emulating Christ's life in all of its aspects; indeed, the stigmatization of St. Francis did a great deal to further the veneration of the Lord's wounds. Doubtless furthered by the prayers composed by St. Claire (d. 1255) and St.

[22] See L. Gougaud, *Dévotions et pratiques ascetiques du Moyen Age* (Paris, 1925), 78-90; R. Berliner,"Arma Christi," *Münchner Jahrbuch der bildenden Kunst,* 6 [1955]: 35-152; L. Réau, *Iconographie de l'art chrétien* (Paris, 1957) *2:* pt. 2, 509ff.; articles on the devotion to and theological significance of the Wounds of Our Lord in *New Catholic Encyclopedia* (New York, 1967), *16:* 1035-1036; R. W. Pfaff, *New Liturgical Feasts in Later Medieval England* (Oxford, 1970), 84-90; G. Schiller, *Iconography of Christian Art* (Greenwich, Conn., 1972), *2:* 190.

[23] Schiller, *Christian Art, 2:* 190; elsewhere Bernard relates the Five Wounds to the five ways Christ's blood was shed (see Berliner, "Arma Christi," 41).

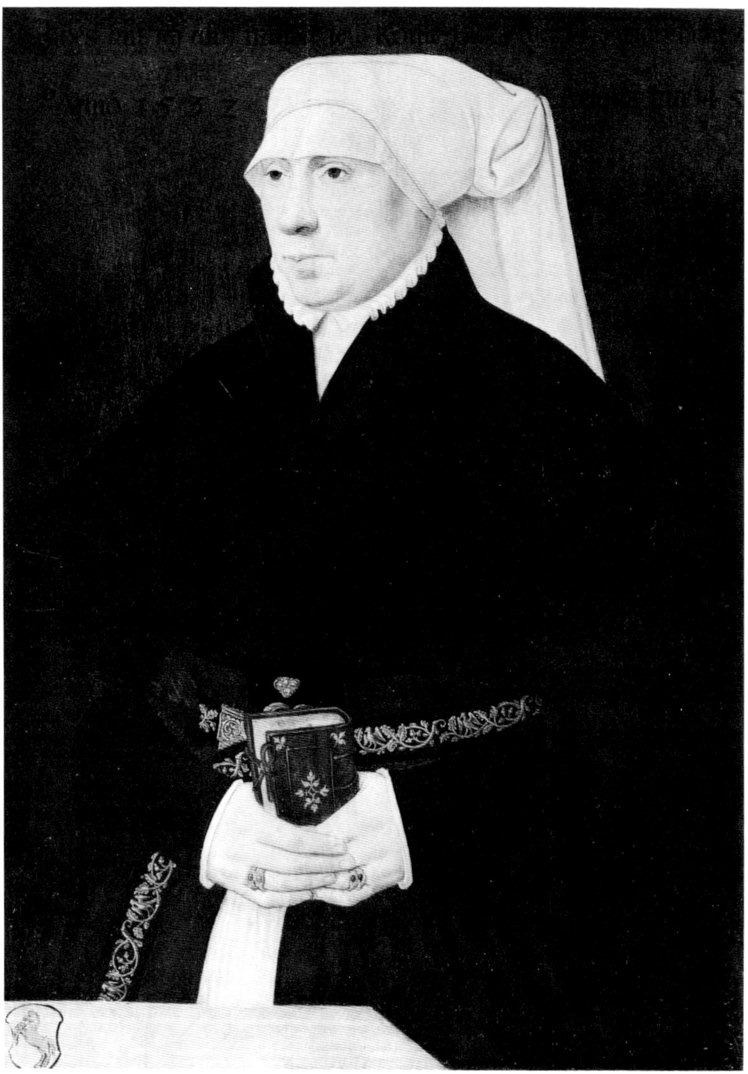

Fig. 10. Ludger tom Ring the Elder, Portrait of a Lady, *1532. Wood. National Gallery of Art, Washington, D.C.; Gift of Chester Dale, 1942*

Gertrude (d. 1302), the devotion to the Five Wounds continued to increase during the second half of the thirteenth century, becoming widespread in the fourteenth and fifteenth centuries. In addition to prayers, the process of dissemination was aided by the many indulgences promised by the Church for the commemoration of the passion and wounds of Christ as well as by an attractive apocryphal legend.[24]

In England devotion to the Five Wounds can be found in manuscripts as early as the late twelfth century but does not seem to have been part of the liturgy. It was not until the early fifteenth century, when the veneration of the Wounds was extremely popular, that a Mass of the Five Wounds was added to English missals to be used at the discretion of the priest or donor of the mass; unlike the Continent, a feast day was never instituted in England.[25] To cite one example from the visual arts, we find the Five Wounds represented

[24] For example, Berliner, "Arma Christi," 49-51, figs. 3, 4, reproduces and discusses a manuscript written in 1320 in the Bibliothèque Royale, Brussels (Ms. 4459-70) which promises forty days indulgence for "commemoratione passionis et armorum ihesu christi."

[25] Pfaff, *Feasts,* 84, 86.

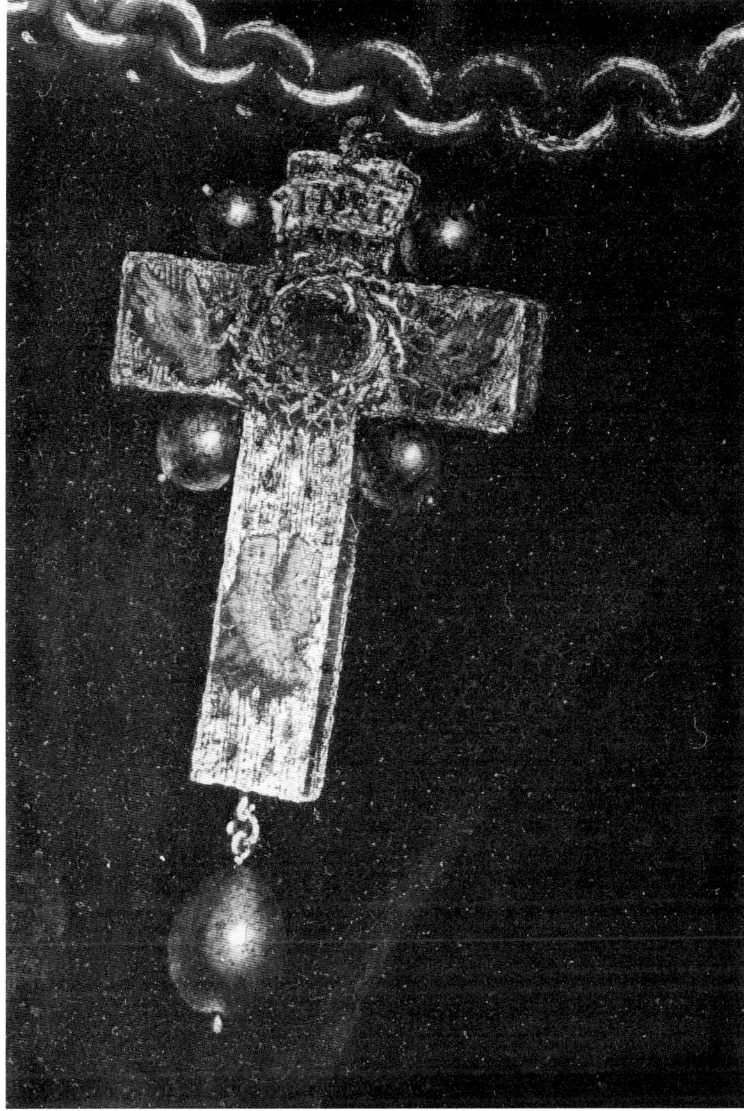

Fig. 11. Hans Holbein the Younger, Sir Brian Tuke *(detail of fig. 2)*

on an early sixteenth-century boss on the church of St. Mary Redcliffe in Bristol (fig. 12).

One explanation of the popularity of the Five Wounds in England is to be found in the supposed restorative powers of this device. For example, an apocryphal legend which often preceded the Mass of the Five Wounds recounts that when Pope Boniface the Second (530-532) was mortally ill, he appealed to God to prolong his life. He was then visited by an angel who told him that if he celebrated the mass five times his health would return.[26]

Having an even more direct bearing on Tuke's crucifix are two gold rings (fig. 13) in the British Museum dating from the late fifteenth or early sixteenth century; the more famous of these is known as the Coventry ring because it was found in Coventry, Warwickshire, in 1802.[27] Around the outside of the ring is engraved the image of Christ standing in the tomb, as well as schematic

[26] Pfaff, *Feasts,* 85; Gougaud, *Dévotions,* 80-81.

[27] O. M. Dalton, *Franks Bequest. Catalogue of the Finger Rings, Early Christian, Byzantine, Teutonic, Mediaeval and Later* (London, 1912), 109, no. 718; C. Oman, *British Rings 800-1914* (London, 1974), cat. no. 69A; British Museum, *Jewellery Through 7000 Years* (London, 1976), cat. no. 371.

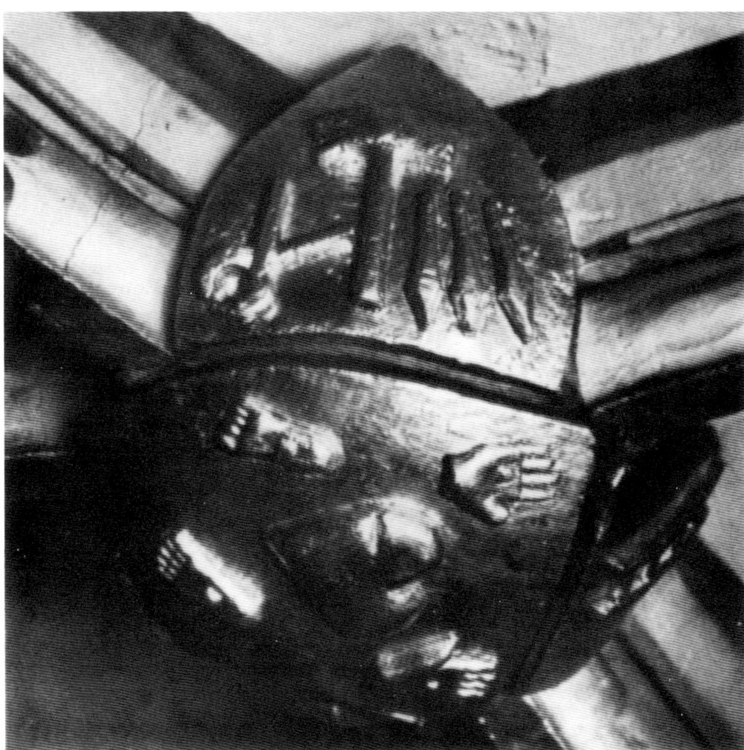

Fig. 12. Detail of boss from the Church of St. Mary Redcliffe, Bristol, England. From Münchner Jahrbuch des bildenden Kunst, *4 (1955): fig. 36*

renderings of the Five Wounds (fig. 14). The Wounds are accompanied by the following inscriptions: *the well of pitty, the well of merci, the well of comfort, the well of gracy,* and *the well of ewer lastingh lyffe.* These are the mystical names given to each of the Wounds, with the words *well of everlasting life* commonly used to describe the large wound in Christ's side. Inside the ring is another inscription:

Wulnera quinq dei sunt medecina mei
crux et passio xti sunt medecina mei jaspar
melchior balthasar ananyzapta, tetragrammaton

The first part of this inscription is undoubtedly derived from a set of verses attached to five prayers that are associated with St. Claire. To wit:

Vulnera quinque Dei (The five wounds of God
Sint medicina mei May they be our healing
Vulneribus quinis By each of the five wounds
Me eruas, Christe, ruinis Deliver us from destruction, O Lord
Da pacem, Christe Give peace, O Lord
Vulneribus quinque[28] By these five wounds)

The second part of the inscription is not religious, but comes from the realm of Renaissance magic. The presumed names of the three Magi—Jaspar (or Caspar), Melchior, and Balthasar—as well as the words *ananyzapta* and *tetragrammaton* were charms or talismans to be invoked against various kinds of illnesses, such as epilepsy, fever, or even intoxication.[29]

[28] Gougaud, *Dévotions,* 81-83; the full text of the prayers can be found in P. Zeffirino Lazzeri, "L'Orazione delle cinque piaghe recitata da S. Chiara," *Archivum Franciscanum historicum, 16* (1923): 246-249. I am deeply indebted to Peter Petkoff for the translation of these verses into English.

[29] Dalton, *Franks Bequest,* 136, no. 870, for ananyzapta; 140, no. 885, for the names of the Three Kings; 109, no. 718, for Tetragrammaton, one of the ten names of God.

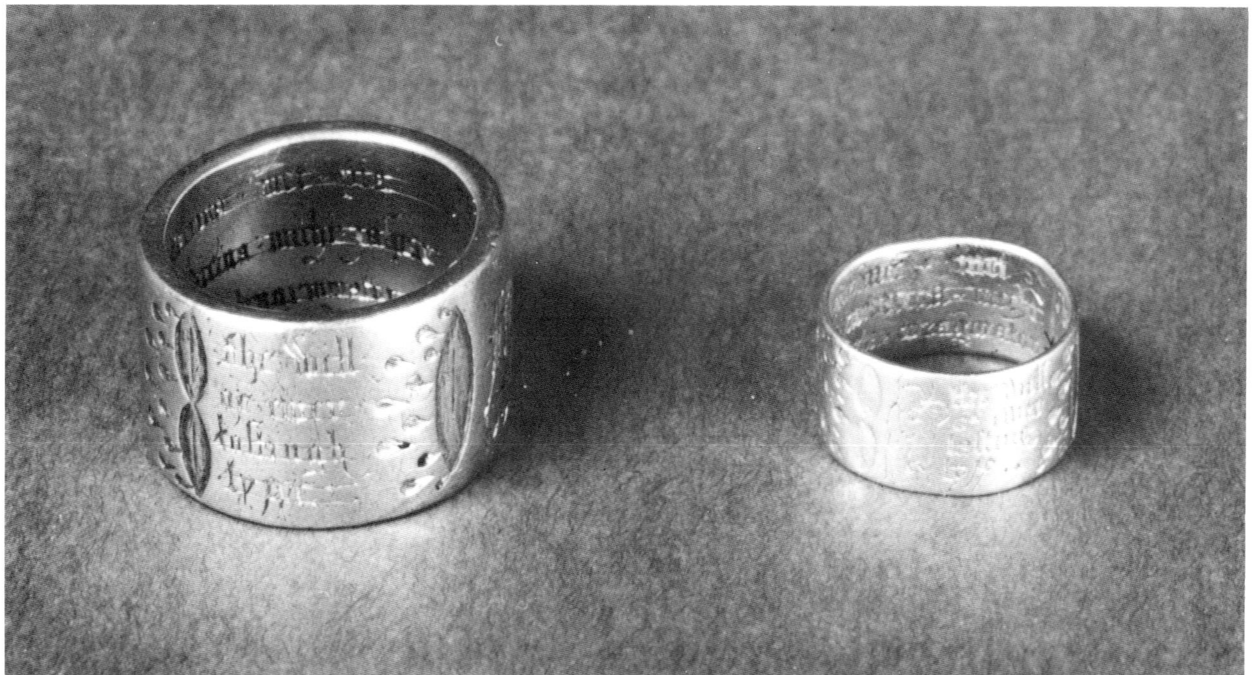

Fig. 13. Gold rings, English, late fifteenth or early sixteenth century. Left: Dalton 718, the Coventry Ring; right: Dalton 719. The British Museum, London

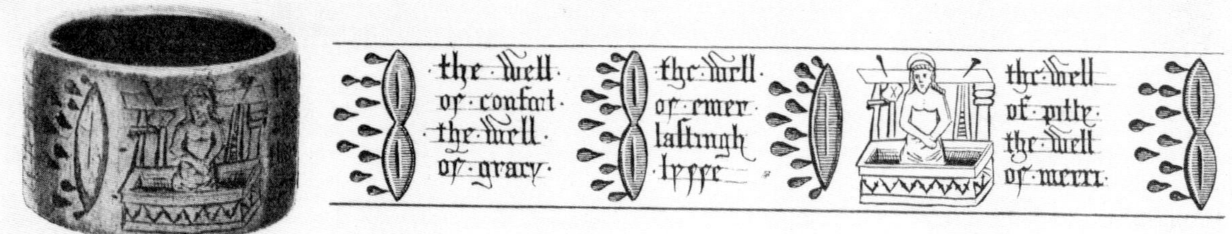

Fig. 14. Rendering of the exterior of the Coventry Ring. From O. M. Dalton, Franks Bequest. Catalogue of the Finger Rings . . . *(London, 1912), 109*

The second ring in the British Museum bears virtually the same inscriptions, but the hoop is engraved with images of the Trinity and the Virgin and Child.[30] That rings of this kind were probably much in demand in the late fifteenth and early sixteenth centuries can be deduced from the instructions contained in the will of Sir Edmund Shaa, who died on March 20, 1487. There it is requested that sixteen gold rings with the well of pity, the well of mercy, and the well of everlasting life, in addition to appropriate images, be made at Shaa's expense.[31]

From the foregoing it is amply evident that the emblem of the Five Wounds of Christ was a prophylactic, especially in conjunction with the prayer *Vulnera quinque Dei,* and was used as a protection against evil, sickness, and even death. There would seem to be no doubt that the crucifix worn by Tuke is the iconographical equivalent of the Coventry ring.[32] In addition it would have had special significance in the year 1528. As we have already mentioned Tuke was appointed treasurer of the king's chamber by mid-April of that year at the latest and on the nineteenth of May, Tuke and Cuthbert, bishop of London,

[30] Dalton, *Franks Bequest,* 110, no. 719; Oman, *British Rings,* cat. no. 69B, identifies the figures as St. John the Baptist, the Trinity, and the Virgin and Child.

[31] The text of the will is quoted by Oman, *British Rings,* cat. no. 69A.

[32] It is, I believe, even possible to see the red gemstone as imbued with a significance beyond that of the wound in the Lord's side. The stone is almost surely a ruby (or intended as one), a gem that is described in medieval lapidaries as both symbolizing Christ as the light of the world and, more germane to our considerations, having the power to drive away sickness and ill conditions. See J. Evans and M. S. Serjeantson, *English Medieval Lapidaries,* Early English Test Society, Original Series, no. 190 (London, 1933), *passim,* esp. 22, 124. Thus the addition of a ruby to Tuke's crucifix would have aided its curative properties. I am indebted to Michael Hitchcock for suggesting this line of investigation and supplying bibliography.

concluded a truce with Margaret of Savoy in conjunction with ambassadors of France. However, in June of 1528 England was struck by a plague that mainly took the form of a severe sweating sickness; it seems to have been concentrated in Great Britain, for it was known in France and Flanders as the king of England's disease.[33]

On the fifth of June, after first explaining that he has fled his house in London because one of his servants is ill, Tuke writes the following to the bishop of London: "The King and my lord Cardinal wish either you or me to come to court for information on certain points about the truce. If I go, I must go in my wagon, which is at my house in Essex, and cannot be here today, for I have a disease *in vesica,* of which Wolsey is aware, and was almost whole; but coming hither from London last night as softly as could be, has made me as ill as before. Besides, I doubt if it would be right to go to the King, having had such a visitor in my house. You could easily satisfy the King. . . . In haste, at Stepney, at 3 o'clock, a.m. in my bed."[34] In another letter Tuke explains that the "wagon" is a cart usually used for his children.[35]

On June 11 Tuke writes from London that he will come to court, but that he is forbidden to ride and therefore will come by water. Were it not for the commandment of the king and Cardinal Wolsey, Tuke would not leave his room, "for stirring is the most dangerous thing I can do, and besides potions and other medecines I am anointed morning and evening, and have other things administered to me not meet to be used in Court."[36]

Sir Brian Tuke was too important to be sick in private, for on June 21 one of Cardinal Wolsey's messengers found him in Waltham, sick of the sweat. Tuke was brought to court astride a mule, but this was done "with marvelous pain; for on my faith I void blood *per virgam.*"[37]

Two days later, Thomas Hennage writes to Wolsey from Henry's court at Hunsdon that "Mr. Tuke is here, and lies in the court under the King's privy chamber, so that he may come at the King's pleasure. At every meal the King sends him a dish from his table."[38]

Tuke continued to suffer from the sweating sickness through the rest of the month of June, and, as best I can ascertain from the documents, he remained seriously ill until at least the middle of July. It is important to keep in mind that because of his own fear of the plague, Henry VIII moved the court from place to place at irregular intervals, disrupting work thoroughly.[39] And if it made life inconvenient for healthy people it must have been torture for Sir Brian Tuke. On the fourteenth of July Tuke wrote a long and famous letter on various aspects of the sweating sickness, noting among other things that "thousands have it from fear, who need not else sweat, especially if they observe good diet." He closes the letter by saying that he "has not strength to write much or study. Writes this at his waking after midnight, fearing to be still for the sweat, with an aching and troubled head."[40]

From the foregoing account we know that Sir Brian Tuke was gravely ill between June 5 and July 14, 1528, and he may well have thought he was going to die. I would propose that Holbein painted Tuke's portrait either during or after Tuke's illness and that the crucifix bearing the Five Wounds of Christ is meant specifically to

[33]For a general discussion of the sickness and the drought and cattle plague that preceded it, see C. W. Ferguson, *Naked to Mine Enemies. The Life of Cardinal Wolsey* (Boston, 1958), 392-395.

[34]*Letters and Papers, 4:* pt. 1, no. 4332.

[35]*Letters and Papers, 4:* pt. 1, no. 4333.

[36]*Letters and Papers, 4:* pt. 1, no. 4358.

[37]*Letters and Papers, 4:* pt. 1, no. 4404.

[38]*Letters and Papers, 4:* pt. 1, no. 4408.

[39]*Letters and Papers, 4:* pt. 1, no. 4440: letter of June 30, 1528 from du Bellay to Montmorency, where we also learn that many of Henry's court had died from the plague within three or four hours, but that of the forty thousand in London who apparently came down with the disease only two thousand died from it.

[40]*Letters and Papers, 4:* pt. 1, no. 4510.

protect against the sweating sickness. While it makes the most sense to date the picture to 1528, to the end of Holbein's first English period, it is conceivable that it might date to the beginning of the second English period, to 1532/33, even though Holbein's clientele had changed.[41] To those who would date the portrait late, I would call attention to the fact that the emblem of the Five Wounds was adopted by those participating in the Pilgrimage of Grace, an uprising in the north of England that occurred in the fall and winter of 1536/37. The protest was directed against Henry's church reforms and called for the return of papal power; it was necessary to call out an army led by the duke of Norfolk to quell the rebellion. It seems inconceivable that Tuke, or anyone else at court, would have worn an emblem of the Five Wounds after 1536 when it would have infuriated and embarrassed the king.[42]

Hans Holbein's portrait of Sir Brian Tuke is a beautifully painted likeness of one of the important figures at the court of Henry VIII, but just as importantly it is a powerful human document. Thanks to his letters we understand more fully why Tuke's visage is pale and wan, his smile faint and pained, and his glance unfocused and melancholy. The final irony is that it was Tuke, the career civil servant, who survived until well into his seventies, outliving his compatriots Wolsey, Wareham, More, and even Holbein. The Tuke we see is a man aware of death as a close and constant companion, and it is he who points to the words from the Book of Job, "Shall not my few days be ended shortly?"

[41]R. Strong, *Holbein and Henry VIII* (London, 1967), 13, emphasizes that Holbein's portrait commissions upon his return to England came from the Steelyard merchants and that it was not until 1537 that Holbein became the king's painter and began to be paid out of the royal accounts. I find merit in Strong's assertion that the lack of royal patronage at the beginning of the second English period may be due to Holbein's previous association with Sir Thomas More and his circle. This, in turn, might be taken to mean that Holbein was more likely to have known Tuke through his association with the More circle than through contact with the court; certainly the early 1530s was not an especially good time to profess friendship with More.

[42]Strong, *Holbein,* 62-63, and the entry on the Pilgrimage of Grace in the *Oxford Dictionary of the Christian Church* (London, 1957), 1073. An embroidered badge from the Pilgrimage of Grace is still in the possession of the duke of Norfolk and is reproduced in F. Steer, "Arundel Castle and its Owners 1067-1660," *The Connoisseur, 197* (Mar. 1978): fig. 8, p. 158.

AUTHOR'S NOTE

During the first week of October 1979, the panel on which *Sir Brian Tuke* was painted was examined by Dr. John Fletcher of the Research Laboratory for Archaeology and Art History, Oxford University, Oxford, England. Based on tree-ring measurements of the edges of the panel, Dr. Fletcher's findings indicate that the likely period for the use of the panel is 1532-1540 and that one of the boards used was probably still growing in 1528, arguing against a date in the first English period.

While Tuke and the crucifix he wears have been of some concern to me for many years, this article had its specific genesis in a lecture given at the National Gallery of Art on May 31, 1978, as part of the events surrounding the inauguration of the East Building. I am thankful to my colleagues at the National Gallery for their supportive yet pungent criticism. In addition to those persons cited in the footnotes, I want to express my gratitude to the staff of the Folger Shakespeare Library for help in making available their incomparable resources; I am also greatly indebted to Sara Campbell, Gisela Goldberg, Yvonne Hackenbroch, Dora Jane Janson, and John Rowlands.

Notes on Two Gabriel de Saint-Aubin Drawings and the Statues They Depict

BETSY JEAN ROSASCO

At the Exposition Universelle held in Paris in 1900, two drawings by Gabriel de Saint-Aubin were exhibited under the title *Le Rendez-Vous aux Tuileries.*[1] One, now in the National Gallery (fig. 1), is a detailed rendering of a statue of a male nude surrounded by some less-finished sketches, including a seated woman in eighteenth-century dress who seems to be waiting for a rendez-vous; this sheet is inscribed, at the base of the statue, "20 may 1774 a 8 heures et demi." The other drawing, in a private collection (fig. 2), is a sketch of a statue of a woman clad in a short tunic.

In his 1931 catalogue of the works of Saint-Aubin, Emile Dacier cast doubt upon the manner in which the drawings had been presented in the exhibition of 1900. He suggested they had been associated arbitrarily and questioned the reference in the title to the Tuileries Gardens.[2] Dacier called the male figure an *Antinous* and the female figure a *Diana;* he compared the latter figure with René Frémin's *Compagne de Diane* in the Louvre, noting significant differences in the pose, however.[3] Despite Dacier's doubts, the vague association with the Tuileries has been repeated in subsequent publications of the drawings under the traditional title; moreover, his identification of the statues has never been reconsidered. I have been able to recognize the subjects of the drawings as known seventeenth-century works. In light of this new identification, I would like to clarify the history and location of these statues, and to discuss the possibility of their influence on later French sculpture.

Two seventeenth-century engravings of statues at Versailles leave no doubt they represent the same compositions sketched by Saint-Aubin. The *Satyr,* engraved by Jean LePautre (fig. 3) and *Hamadryade,* engraved by François Chauveau (fig. 4), are designated as works by the royal sculptor Louis Lerambert, part of a series of Satyrs and Bacchantes commissioned in 1665. Carved of stone and measuring seven Ancien Régime feet in height, the four figures by

1 The drawings were most recently exhibited together in the exhibition *France in the Eighteenth Century,* London, Royal Academy, 1968, nos. 629, 630. The former (black crayon heightened with pen strokes; 22.4 x 14.6 cm. [8 13/16 x 5 3/4 in]), now in the National Gallery of Art (Rosenwald Collection, B-22,305), is first mentioned alone in the Marquis de Fourquevaux sale held in Paris Dec. 15-16, 1876, as no. 30. The two drawings appeared together in the A. Beurdeley sale (Paris, Mar. 13-15, 1905, no. 222) and in the Jean Dubois sale (Paris, Mar. 21-22, 1927, no. 66). In addition to the Exposition Universelle *Rétrospective de la Ville de Paris* (no. 265), they were shown together at the Galerie Cailleux in Paris in 1951 (*Le Dessin Français de Watteau à Prud'hon,* no. 138-9). I thank Mrs. Suzanne Folds McCullagh and M. Jean Cailleux for generously making the photograph in fig. 2 available to me.

2 Emile Dacier, *Gabriel de Saint-Aubin, Peintre, Dessinateur, et Graveur (1724-1780)* (Paris-Brussels, 1931), 2: 95, nos. 543-544.

3 Frémin's figure is illustrated in Louis Réau, "Les Compagnes de Diane," *Gazette des Beaux-Arts,* 6th s., 7 (1932): 143, fig. 7.

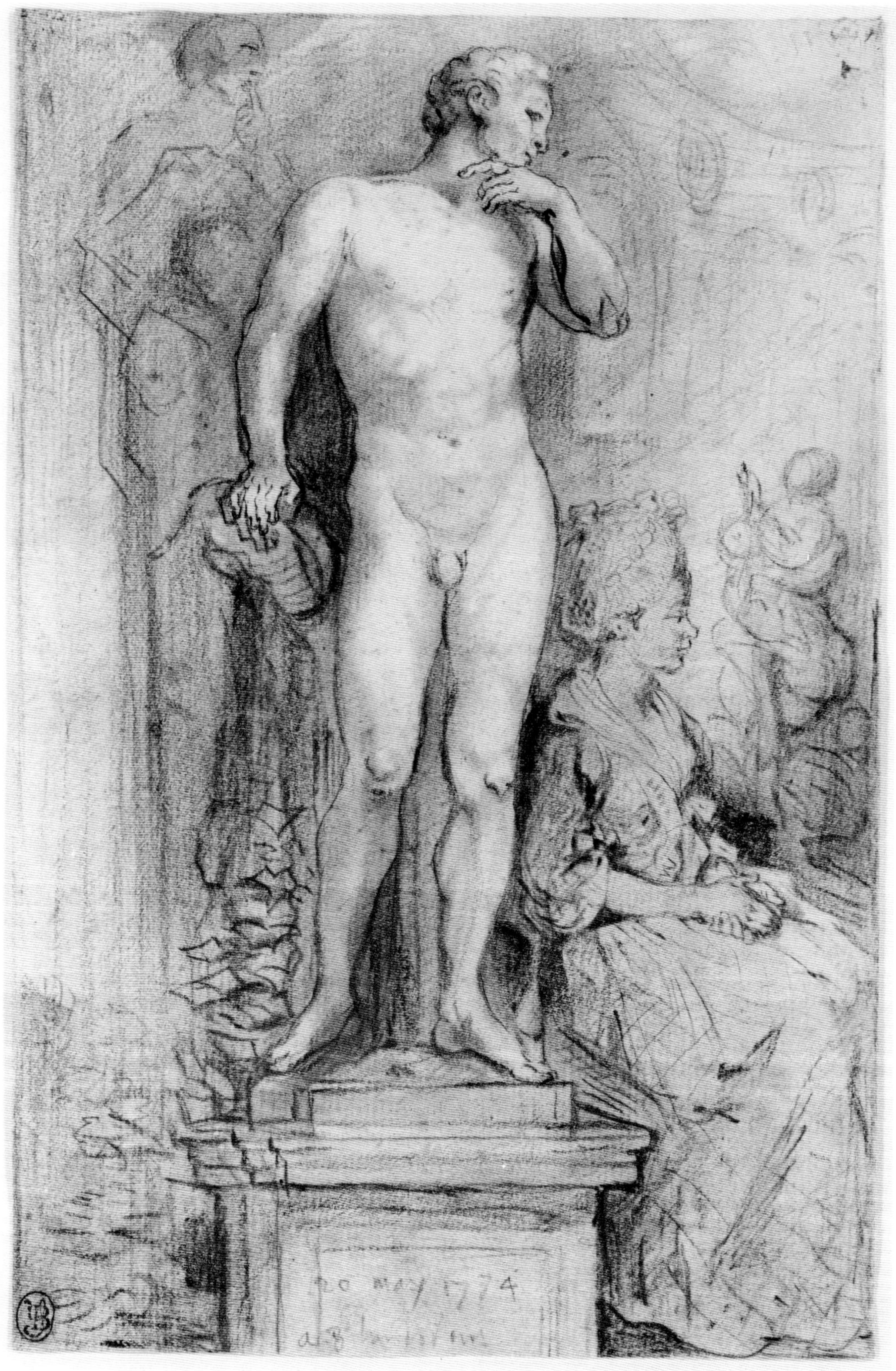

Fig. 1. Gabriel de Saint-Aubin, The Rendez-Vous in a Park, *1774. Black crayon heightened with pen strokes on paper. National Gallery of Art, Washington, D.C.; Rosenwald Collection*

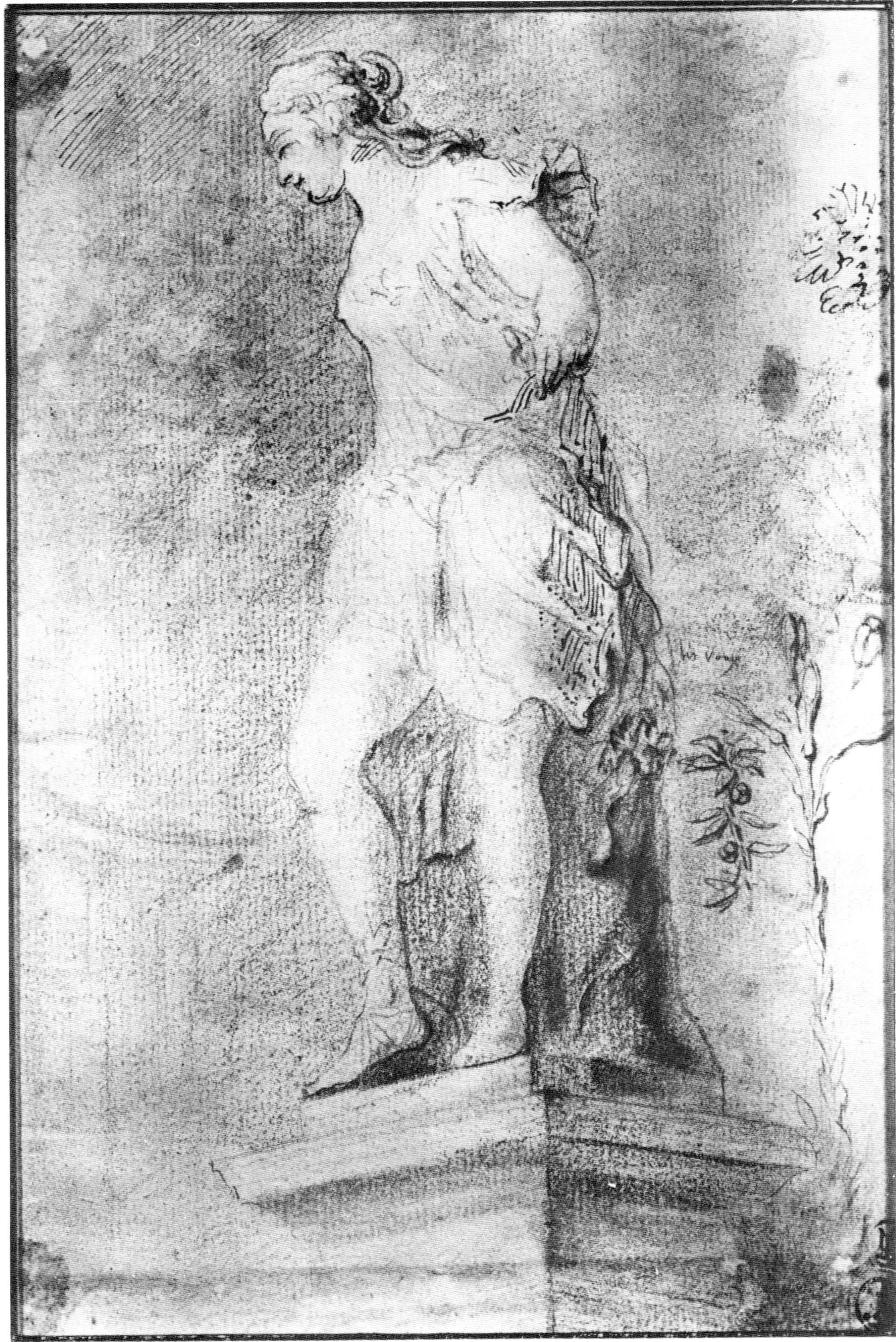

Fig. 2. Gabriel de Saint-Aubin, Statue of a Dancing Figure. *Black crayon heightened with pen and ink. Private Collection. Photograph: courtesy of M. Jean Cailleux*

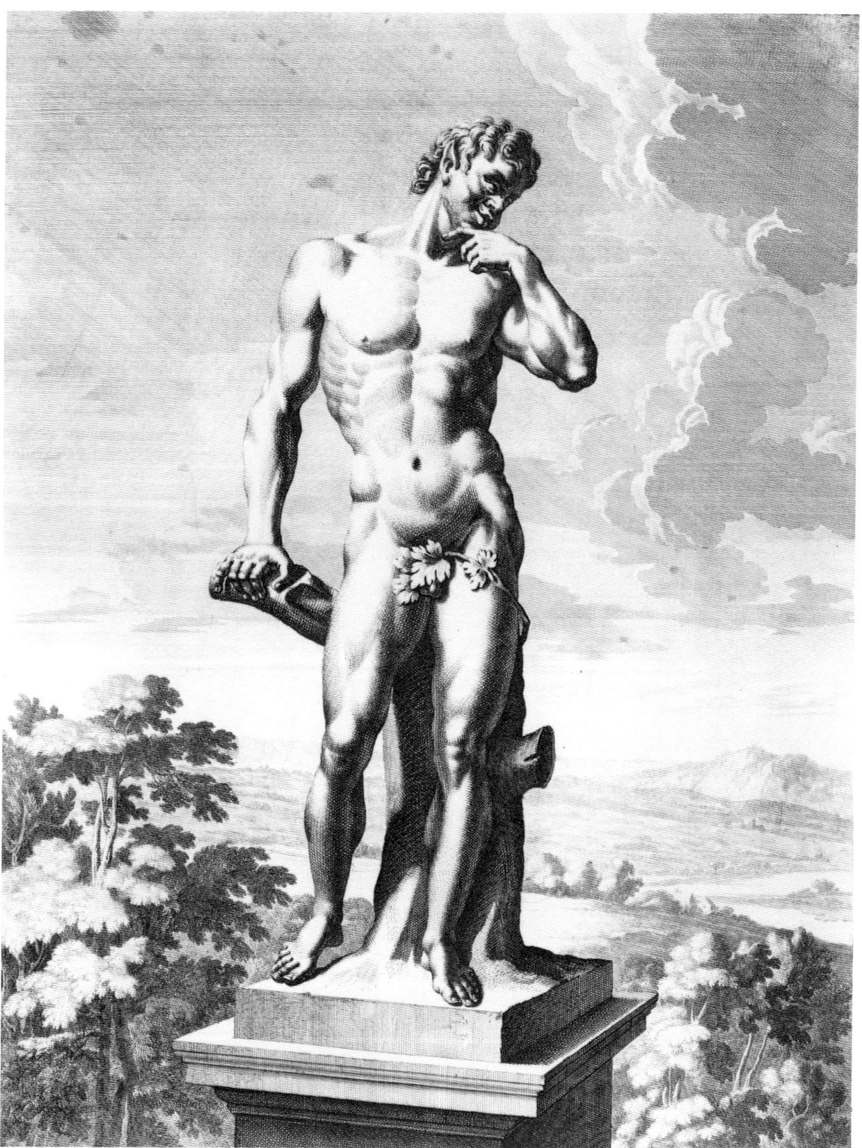

Fig. 3. Jean LePautre. Statue d'un Faune. . ., *1672. Engraving after a statue of Louis Lerambert. From* Cabinet du roi. *Prints Division, The New York Public Library, Astor, Lenox and Tilden Foundations*

Lerambert and four others by his colleague Philippe de Buyster were the earliest decorations of the Grande Rondeau of Versailles, the basin which later became the Bassin d'Apollon.[4] We owe the existence of the engravings of LePautre and Chauveau to the project to publish illustrations of the statues in the French royal collection, the so-called *Cabinet du Roi* of 1679.

The Satyrs and Bacchantes were removed from the gardens of Versailles even before the end of the seventeenth century. As the country château took on the character of a royal residence in the 1670s and 1680s, and the gardens were enriched with sculptures in the noble materials of marble and bronze, the early stone and lead groups were systematically replaced. The Lerambert and Buyster works remained in the gardens only until 1692; then, when the king's brother, Philippe, duc d'Orléans, was renovating the Palais-Royal,

[4] Jules Guiffrey, ed., *Comptes des Bâtiments du Roi sous le règne de Louis XIV* (Paris, 1881), *1:* 79: "22 may 1665-24 avril 1666: à Philippe Buister, sculpteur, pour les quatre figures qu'il a faites autour du grand rondeau de Versailles (4 p.) . . . 1300#. 22 may 1665-29 janvier 1666: à Louis Lerambert, sculpteur, pour les quatre figures de pierre qu'il a faites et posées autour du grand rondeau (5 p.) . . . 1400#. "On this commission see Pierre de Nolhac, "Les Premiers Sculpteurs de Versailles," *Gazette des Beaux-Arts,* 3rd s., *21* (1899): 89-100. In his 1681 description of Versailles, Combes wrote, "Autour de cette Fontaine, proche le Canal, sont posées huit Statuës de pierre, faites par

his new residence in Paris, Louis XIV made him a present of the eight stone figures.[5] We know the date of their placement in the gardens of the Palais-Royal: in the biography of Louis Lerambert, read before the Académie Royale de Peinture et de Sculpture on March 7, 1693, the statues were said to be at the Palais-Royal "depuis un mois."[6]

In 1730, the garden of the Palais-Royal was redesigned by Claude Desgotz, the nephew of André LeNôtre and a landscape architect in his own right. The statues from Versailles were reused in the newly refurbished garden; they can be recognized in drawings and were still considered worthy of mention in guides to Paris.[7] Writing in 1752, Germain Brice qualified them as works "d'une assez bonne main."[8] Another text of the mid-eighteenth century, while retaining the name of Lerambert as their author, alluded to their material as stucco;[9] clearly exposure to the elements for nearly a century had taken its toll on the stone.

In 1781, the duc de Chartres (the future Philippe Egalité) commissioned the architect Victor Louis to construct new wings enclosing the garden of the Palais-Royal. During the course of this work the statues in the garden were removed, as is proved by a payment of 1782.[10] Unfortunately no documents concerning their subsequent fate have come to light. This brief history of the Lerambert statues shows, however, that Saint-Aubin sketched them while they decorated the garden of the Palais-Royal, eight years before their removal. Emile Dacier's assumption that the drawings are unrelated is erroneous; they should be considered a pair. His inference that they bear no relation to the Tuileries Gardens is correct, and they might better be referred to as *Le Rendez-Vous au Palais-Royal.*

IT REMAINS TO COMMENT on the interesting choice of subject matter by a draftsman of the Louis XVI period. Gabriel de Saint-Aubin, an *habitué* of art salesrooms, is an artist whose marginal sketches in auction catalogues provide precious evidence of the taste of collectors of his age. In the drawings under discussion, we find him choosing to sketch works in a Parisian park which had both an historical interest, as remnants of the early sculptural decoration of Versailles, and a value as examples of the art of a master of the previous century whose reputation remained high but whose works were rare. We can also infer that these particular compositions of Lerambert contained stylistic traits that appealed to the eighteenth-century artist since we detect a strong "proto-eighteenth-century" current in both the statues Saint-Aubin chose to draw. In his monograph on the early eighteenth-century sculptor Antoine Coysevox, Luc Benoist suggested Lerambert and Buyster's 1665 cycle for Versailles was an important source for the subject matter of Coysevox's *Faune* and *Hamadryade* made for the gardens of Marly between 1706 and 1710.[11] I would extend this observation to the formal level: analogies between the works of Lerambert and some early eighteenth-century sculptures by a younger generation of sculptors, similarities thus far overlooked, may be even more significant for the history of French sculpture. One example is of particular interest in our context since it concerns a statue in the National Gallery.

We have mentioned that Emile Dacier saw similarities between the statue of a woman sketched by Saint-Aubin, which he entitled *Diana* (fig. 2) and René Frémin's *Compagne de Diane* (1710-1717), likewise a statue of an active female figure dressed in a short garment and captured in an open pose. An even closer comparison can be made between Lerambert's *Hamadryade* (fig. 4) and another statue in the

le sieur le Rembert: Ce sont des Satyrs & des Bacantes de la Compagnie de Baccus, elles sont faites à plaisir, & pour servir d'ornement à ce grand Bassin." (*Explication historique de ce qu'il y a de plus remarquable dans la maison royale de Versailles* [Paris, 1681], 103.) The *Hamadryade* is depicted in the background of the portrait of Lerambert by N.-A.S. Belle (illustrated in Pierre de Nolhac, *Les Jardins de Versailles* [Paris, 1906], 76).

5 Victor Champier and G.-Roger Sandoz, *Le Palais-Royal d'après des Documents Inédits, (1629-1900)* (Paris, 1900), *1*: 175ff.

6 Guillet de Saint-Georges, "Louis Lerambert," in Louis Dussieux et al., eds., *Mémoires Inédits sur la Vie et les Ouvrages des Membres de l'Académie Royale de Peinture et de Sculpture* (Paris, 1854), *1*: 333.

7 Champier and Sandoz, *Le Palais-Royal, 1*: 345.

8 Germain Brice, *Description de la Ville de Paris et de tout ce qu'elle contient de plus remarquable,* ed. Pierre Codet, (Paris, 1752; Paris, 1971), 78.

9 Cited in J. Vatout, *Souvenirs Historiques des Résidences Royales de France* (Paris, 1838), *2*: 145.

10 Champier and Sandoz, *Le Palais-Royal, 1*: 435.

11 Luc Benoist, *Coysevox* (Paris, 1930), 13.

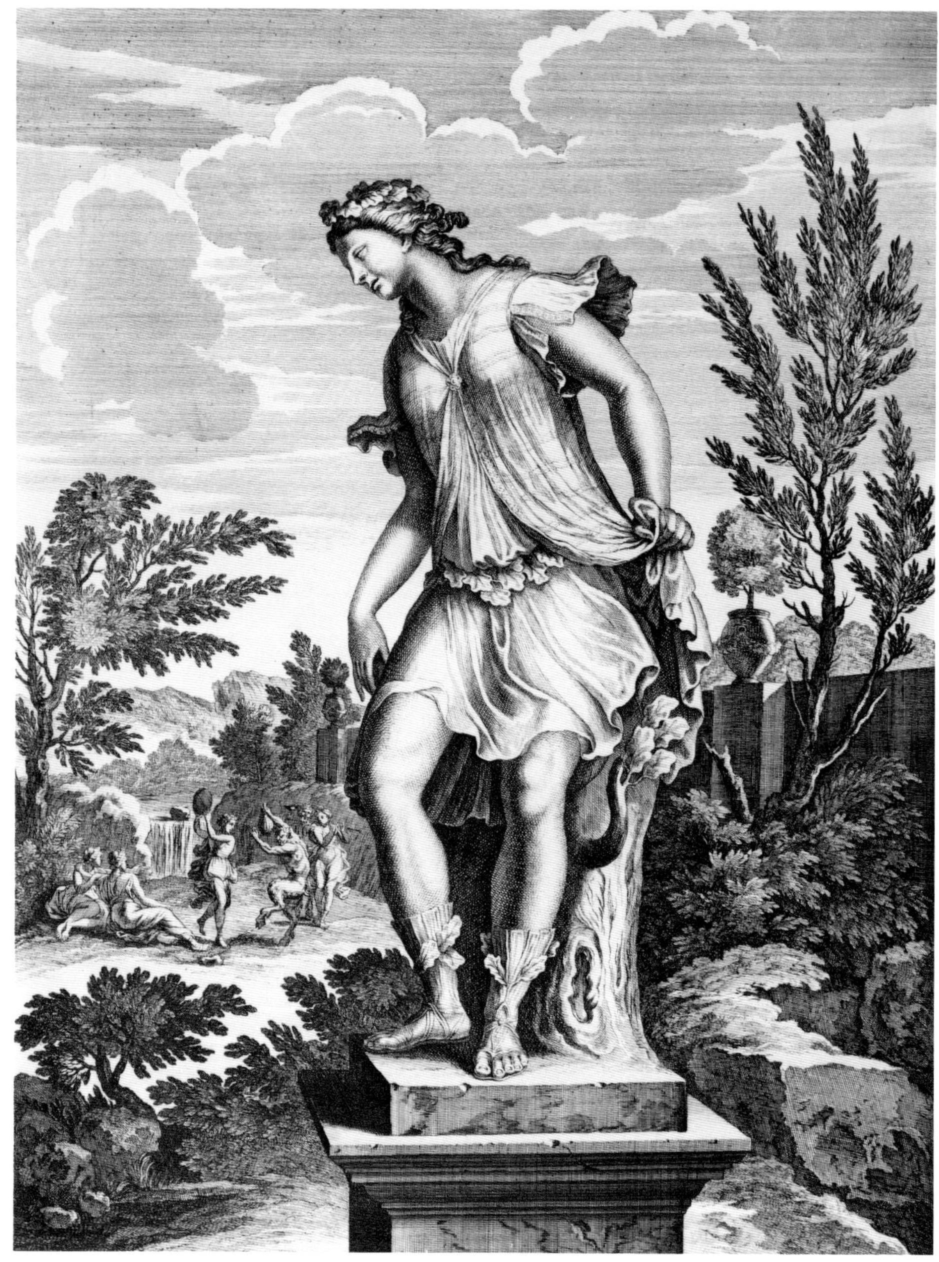

Fig. 4. François Chauveau. Statue d'une Danseuse. . ., *1675. Engraving after a statue of Louis Lerambert. From* Cabinet du Roi. *Prints Division, The New York Public Library; Astor, Lenox and Tilden Foundations*

series of Compagnes de Diane, the figure by Jean-Louis LeMoyne, completed between 1710 and 1724 and now in the National Gallery (fig. 5).[12] The resemblance between the two figures can hardly be fortuitous. LeMoyne has modified the contraposto of Lerambert's figure to some extent, to be sure. The head of LeMoyne's figure is now turned toward the supporting leg, and the left arm crosses the body to create a serpentine line reminiscent of sixteenth-century Italian models, especially in the oeuvre of Giambologna. Reinterpreted though it may be, the figure of Lerambert nonetheless remains

[12] Jean-Louis LeMoyne, *Compagne de Diane,* 1724. Màrble; 182.5 x 076.5 x 057.8 cm (71¾ x 30⅛ x 22¾ in). National Gallery of Art, Widener Collection, A-127.

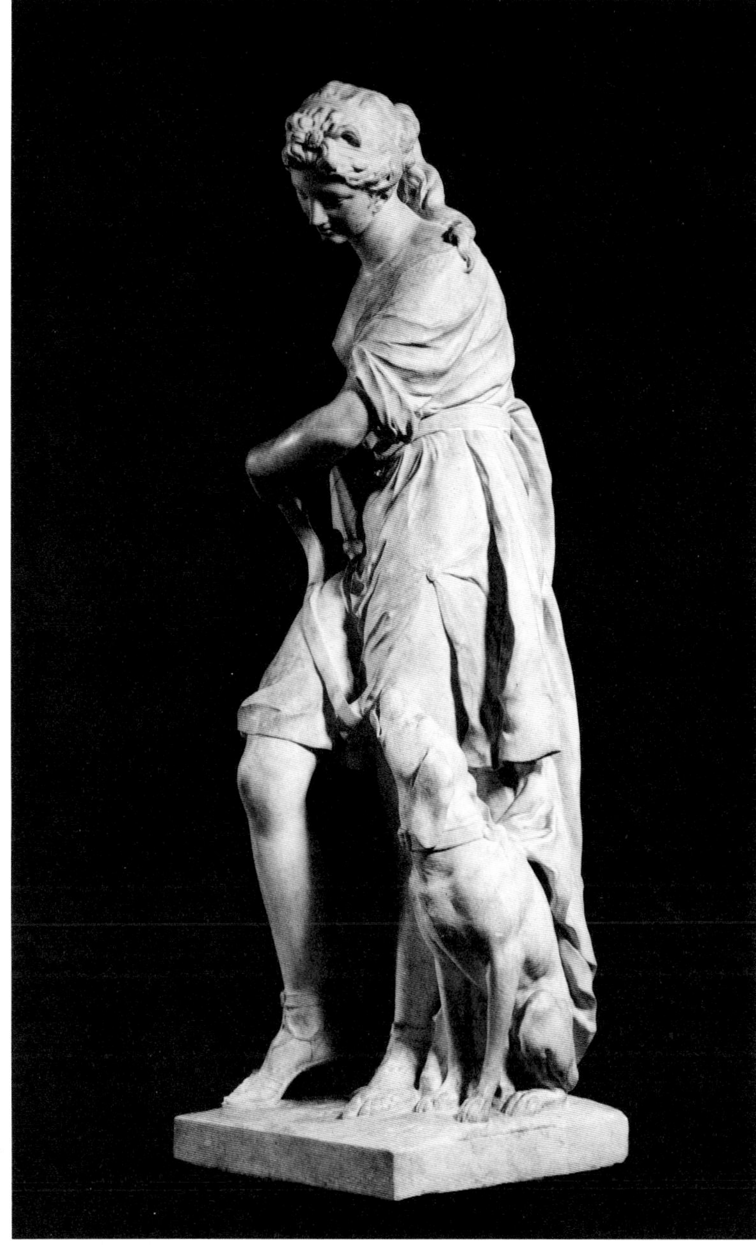

Fig. 5. Jean-Louis LeMoÿne, A Companion of Diana, *1724. Marble. National Gallery of Art, Washington, D.C.; Widener Collection*

the obvious source for LeMoyne's composition, for the half-raised leg and the overall expressive qualities closely follow their seventeenth-century model.[13] Where indeed but in the works of the first sculptors of Versailles could LeMoyne have found precedents for such a lilting posture, for such gaiety and rustic grace?

[13] The "dancing" posture of Lerambert's figure is no doubt derived from the famous *Satyr* from the Florentine grand ducal collection of antiquities, a figure who raises his foot to beat time with a *kroupezion* (cf. Margarete Bieber, *The Sculpture of the Hellenistic Age,* 2nd ed. [New York, 1967], fig. 562). We should also mention other possible instances of influence of Lerambert's figures on the sculptures of the early eighteenth century; both Robert LeLorrain's *Bacchus* and Sébastien Slodtz's lost *Vertumne,* figures of 1710 and 1706, rested one hand on a tree trunk in the same gesture as that of Lerambert's *Faune* (cf. Christiane Pinatel, *Les Sculptures Antiques des Jardins de Versailles* [Paris, 1963], pl. XIX; and François Souchal, *Les Slodtz, Sculpteurs et Décorateurs du Roi, (1685-1764)* [Paris, 1967], pl. 7, b).

Winslow Homer's *Right and Left*

JOHN WILMERDING

Beyond the occasional museum bulletin or scholarly journal essay, there are surprisingly few articles devoted to comprehensive examinations of single important paintings by major American artists. Significant works, to be sure, have received discussion in the larger contexts of an artist's career or of certain focal themes. Even more rare is the monograph published on a single work of American art. Only in Viking's Art in Context series does one find modest volumes treating single works, though just one has been given to an American painting. That was *Trumbull: The Declaration of Independence* (New York, 1976), by Irma Jaffe; and, ironically, we must note that this subject has greater interest for its historical rather than artistic qualities.

When we turn to the art of Winslow Homer, unequivocally one of America's greatest painters, we discover that virtually no major work by him has been the focus of an entire extended study. The one notable exception has been Nicolai Cikovsky's article, "Winslow Homer's *Prisoners from the Front,*" for the *Metropolitan Museum Journal* in 1977.[1] It is all the more paradoxical, therefore, that this artist's possibly greatest work, his late masterpiece *Right and Left* (fig. 1),[2] has had no such attention. It, of course, finds its rightful place in all surveys of American art and in often perceptive discussion in the Homer biographies. Yet the only two published commentaries given to this work alone are based on press releases provided by the National Gallery of Art. The first dates from the time *Right and Left* was acquired in 1951, and the second from 1958, when the large Homer retrospective opened at the Gallery and the artist's market reputation was soaring. These pieces for *Art Digest* and *Newsweek* were respectively titled: "The Thanksgiving Dinner was Spoiled," and "Better than Apple Pie."[3]

1 Nicolai Cikovsky, Jr., "Winslow Homer's *Prisoners from the Front,*" *Metropolitan Museum Journal, 12* (1977): 155-172.

2 Oil on canvas, 71.8 x 122.9 cm (28¼ x 48⅜ in); National Gallery of Art no. 1067, gift of the Avalon Foundation.

3 "The Thanksgiving Dinner Was Spoiled," *Art Digest,* Sept. 15, 1957, 41; and "Better than Apple Pie," *Newsweek,* Nov. 24, 1958, 78. For an almost complete Homer bibliography see Melinda Dempster Davis, *Winslow Homer: An Annotated Bibliography of Periodical Literature* (Metuchen, N.J., 1975).

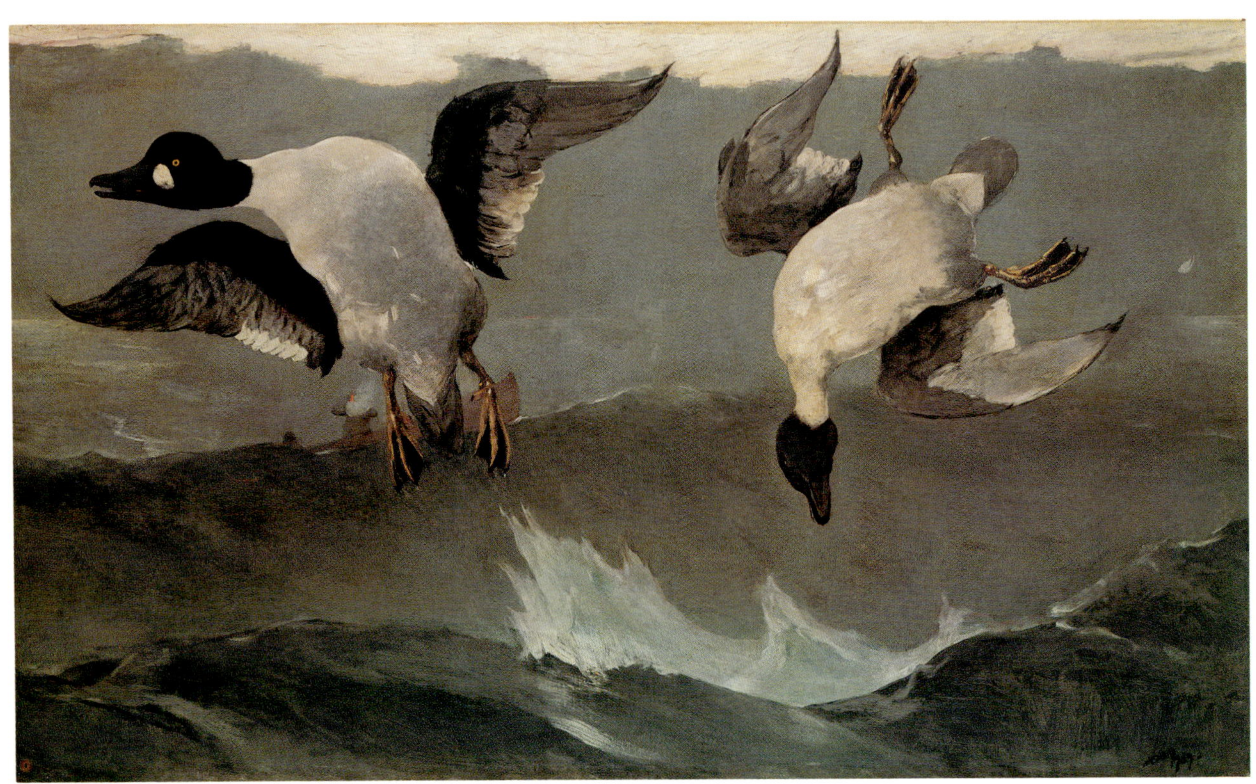

Fig. 1. Winslow Homer, Right and Left, *1909. Oil on canvas. National Gallery of Art, Washington, D.C.; Gift of the Avalon Foundation 1951*

One of the most imaginative appraisals of the painting came at the conclusion of a larger discussion of American works by Roger B. Stein, selected as proposed indices to periods of national culture.[4] In his essay Stein draws our attention to the almost Whistlerian harmonies characterizing the restrained tonal variations of *Right and Left,* as well as the apparent discord in the composition's spatial ambiguity. In this latter regard he reminds us of the viewer's unnatural positioning over water, in relationship to the victimized ducks in the foreground, and our uneasy awareness of threatened and brutal disorder. Forcing us to contrast the visual beauties of form in this painting with its aggressive content of death and chaos, Stein argues that this discordance offers an insight to America itself on the threshold of a new century with all its social, political, and intellectual upheavals impending. The persuasiveness of his argument is strengthened when we read of Henry Adams' anxieties about the loosed energies of a new age in his *Education,* from the same years, or look into the elegaic faces of Thomas Eakins' late portraits, or meditate on the mortal remains of worn books and private mementoes in John F. Peto's still-life gatherings.

[4] Roger B. Stein, "Structure as Meaning: Towards a Cultural Interpretation of American Painting," *American Art Review,* 3, no. 2 (Mar.-Apr. 1976): 66-78.

Right and Left indeed possesses a subtle near-monochromy of color, as Stein argues—though actually it is more gray-green than blue and brown. This muted, opaque palette is at first glance strangely unassuming; at the same time, the looming birds appear immediately assertive, still and solid as sculptures, fixed and arbitrary as a still life. This disjunction between calm and boldness gains in expressive power as we begin to explore the crucial factors of the size, shape, and placement of the two ducks. Homer's manipulation of such pictorial issues found perhaps its most original resolution in this painting, which was literally the culmination of a life's work and creative thought.

William Howe Downes, Homer's first biographer, tells how in the fall of 1908, when the painting was begun,[5] Homer went out in a boat with a friend to observe him firing a shotgun at birds and their positions as they were shot. The artist's nephew, Charles L. Homer, recounted a slightly different narrative to Phillip Beam, to the effect that Homer watched from the Prout's Neck cliffs while his friend Will Googins fired blanks up the cliffs from a rowboat offshore.[6] Certainly, the idea of birds in air as a large still-life design had some precedents in Homer's own previous work, though *Right and Left* is by far his most provocative composition in its placement of the viewer in the line of fire with the ducks. This singular confrontation with mortality is surely a key element in the painting's powerful effect on us.

[5] Phillip C. Beam, *Winslow Homer at Prout's Neck* (Boston, 1966), 248.

[6] William Howe Downes, *The Life and Works of Winslow Homer* (Boston and New York, 1911), 245; and Beam, *Homer,* 249. Beam also modifies the account of Homer's getting the birds, stating that a Boston friend, Phineas W. Sprague, had been duck hunting at the Neck in the fall of 1908 and hung a pair of ducks on the artist's studio door.

Downes asserts, however, that Homer came to paint this subject when he purchased some ducks for his Thanksgiving dinner.[7] A long-time hunter himself, Homer had many times previously painted hunting subjects, including several devoted to wild birds, along with the other well-known sporting themes depicting deer, bear, and fish. It is not surprising then that the handsome plumage of these Thanksgiving birds might lure him into arranging and studying them for a new canvas. Indeed, the holiday passed without the ducks ever reaching Homer's table, for he was hard at work on his oil of them when he wrote his brother Charles about it on December 8:

[7] Downes, *Homer,* 244-245. Downes apparently confused his years, reporting that the occasion was in Nov. 1909, when it seems fairly certain that Homer began this work in the previous autumn and completed it early in the new year of 1909.

I do not think I shall leave here before January—then I shall go directly south to Homosassa after about three days in New York.

I am painting when it is light enough—on a most surprising picture but the days are short & sometimes very dark—

I am very well—but how are you & Mattie—

Affectionately
Winslow[8]

[8] Transcript of letter to Charles Homer in files of the National Gallery of Art, Washington. Historians generally agree that the picture referred to here can only be *Right and Left,* since Homer was working on no other known painting at the time ("in maturity he averaged only two or three oils a year"—Lloyd Goodrich, *Winslow Homer* [New York, 1959], 31) and since indeed the painting is "surprising" within his oeuvre. See Beam, *Homer,* 247-248, and Lloyd Goodrich, *Winslow Homer* (New York, 1944), 197-198.

Once involved in this, even for him, "surprising" composition, Homer must have sensed that it would take several weeks of steady work; indeed he did not finish it until January 7, when he dated it with the new year, 1909, and prepared to leave for Florida.

The suggestion of life and death held in vivid balance was a theme preoccupying Homer throughout his mature career. But such a juxtaposition appears to have grown out of a much larger and more complex pattern of pairings, both formal and iconographic, occurring in his art. Homer's imagery, drawn as it is from anecdotal events, nonetheless reflects a consistent pattern of selection and arrangement that demonstrates the artist's ongoing concern for structure. The formula of pairs especially falls within this pattern and allowed Homer to explore certain relationships. While he could represent the people and objects seen in a pleasing or harmonious arrangement, he could also introduce or reinforce the sense of separation among groupings that pairs imply. In his most intriguing compositions, he was able to use the pairing formula not only to show separation but also to imply oppositions.

Some Homer works simply convey an image of paired shapes or figures: children playing in a field, men hunting in the woods together, women promenading side by side on the beach, trout leaping from a stream. In other instances the forms convey both an image and an implication of various degrees of oppositions and polarities, such as male versus female, one animal against another, water striking rock, man battling nature. This instinct of Homer's for paired figures and opposed forces begins early in his work and is readily evident in his illustrations drawn for *Harper's Weekly* magazine and other journals. Although he easily composed multifigured compositions, it is surprising how regularly he drew just two individuals and made them the dominant focus of his stronger graphic designs.

One of Homer's best-known early graphics is the Civil War engraving known as *The Army of the Potomac–A Sharpshooter,* appearing in *Harper's,* November 16, 1862. Although a soldier is shown up in a tree, he is presented close-up, taking aim at some enemy out of our frame of vision, and this striking opposition of seen and unseen combattants is the primary reason for this image's dramatic force. More straightforward are the various courtship pairings he drew for illustrations throughout that decade.[9] There is another series depicting youths at leisure, in single or multiple pairs,[10] and there are several devoted to men working or hunting in the Adirondacks woods.[11] One can also find numerous counterparts to these images among Homer's pencil and charcoal drawings of the 1870s and eighties, for example, those showing children playing on swings or sitting on fences and young women walking together. In one elaborate sequence Homer sketched a pair of youths carrying, variously, a bucket of clams or berries between them; this underwent a

[9] For example, *Our Watering Places–The Empty Sleeve at Newport* in *Harper's Weekly,* Aug. 26, 1865; *Thanksgiving Day–Hanging Up the Musket* in *Frank Leslie's Illustrated News Paper,* Dec. 23, 1865; *St. Valentine's Day–The Old Story in All Lands* in *Harper's Weekly,* Feb. 22, 1868; *You Are Really Picturesque, My Love* in *The Galaxy,* June 1868; *All in the Gay and Golden Weather* in *Appleton's Journal of Literature, Science, and Art,* June 16, 1869; *The Artist in the Country* in *Appleton's Journal,* June 19, 1869; *Come* in *The Galaxy,* Sept. 1869; *Weary and Dissatisfied with Everything* in *The Galaxy,* Nov. 1869; *A Quiet Day in the Woods* in *Appleton's Journal,* June 25, 1870. See Barbara Gelman, *The Wood Engravings of Winslow Homer* (New York, 1969); and Lloyd Goodrich, *The Graphic Art of Winslow Homer* (Washington, D.C., 1968).

[10] *Swinging on a Birch Tree* in *Our Young Folks,* June 1867; *Summer in the Country* in *Appleton's Journal,* July 10, 1869; *The Playmates* in *Our Young Folks,* Nov. 1869; *Making Hay* in *Harper's Weekly,* July, 6, 1872; *The Noon Recess* in *Harper's Weekly,* June 28, 1873; *The Bathers* in *Harper's Weekly,* Aug. 16, 1873.

[11] *Danger Ahead* in *Appleton's Journal,* Apr. 30, 1870; *Trapping in the Adirondacks* in *Every Saturday,* Dec. 24, 1870; *Deer Stalking in the Adirondacks in Winter* in *Every Saturday,* Jan. 21, 1871; *Lumbering in Winter* in *Every Saturday,* Jan. 28, 1871; *Camping Out in the Adirondacks Mountains* in *Harper's Weekly,* Nov. 7, 1874.

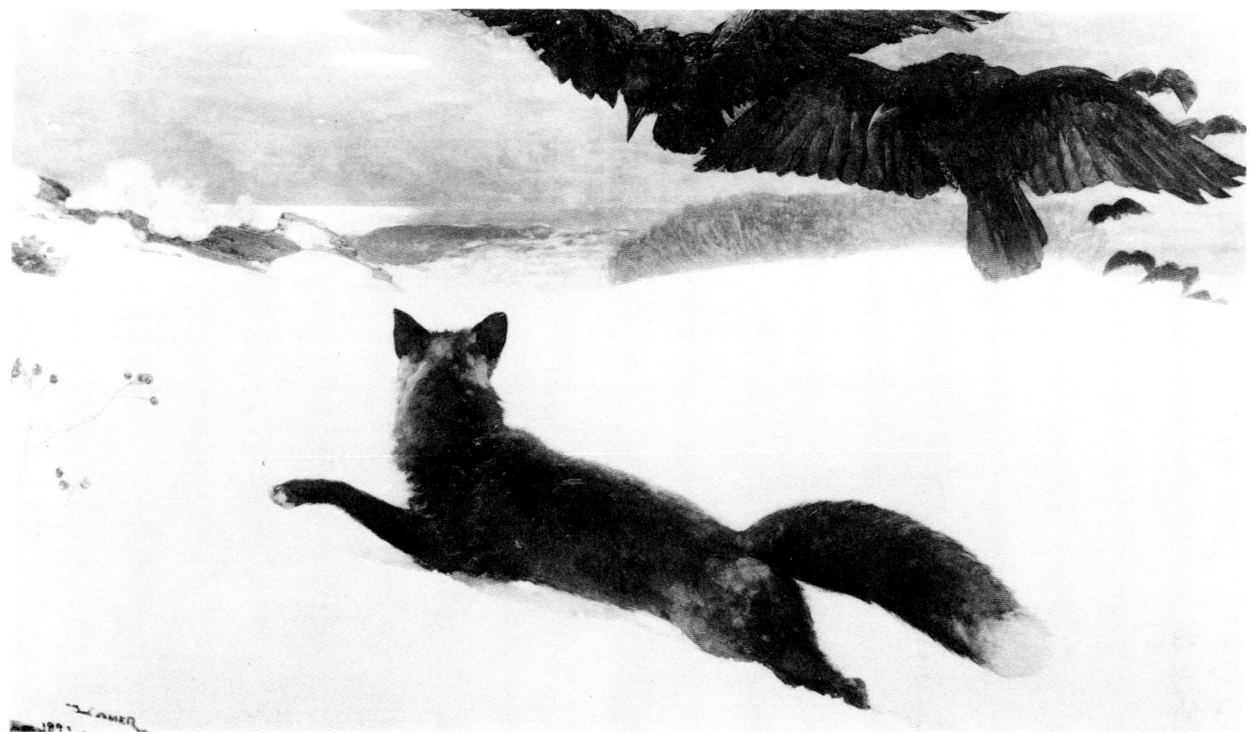

Fig. 2. Winslow Homer, The Fox Hunt, *1893. Oil on canvas. Pennsylvania Academy of the Fine Arts, Philadelphia*

number of metamorphoses in drawings, wood engravings, watercolors, and oils.

Through his paintings, Homer could explore the pairing formula still more fully, and one can trace the resulting themes quite readily. For example, with *Boys in a Pasture* (1874; Museum of Fine Arts, Boston) the subject is the simple, light-hearted representation of children in pairs; and in *Weaning the Calf* (1875; North Carolina Museum of Art, Raleigh), Homer pairs both children and animals as well as various landscape elements. Homer developed differing moods around his depictions of women. In one serene and uncomplicated image, *Long Branch, New Jersey* (1869; Museum of Fine Arts, Boston), two women both constitute the pairing and provide the contrast (one's parasol is up, the other's is down). In other examples, *The Cotton Pickers* (1876; Los Angeles County Museum) and *Promenade on the Beach* (1880; Museum of Fine Arts, Springfield, Massachusetts) the mood is shifted from the serene to the somber—even threatening—and an element of surrealism is added.

In some canvases, paired males interact with nature, or male and female pairs fight against natural forces in a battle for survival.[12] In still other works a lone figure and a natural phenomenon constitute the pairing;[13] or, as in *Northeaster* (1895; Metropolitan Museum of Art, New York) and *The Fox Hunt* (1893; fig. 2) differing elements of nature are locked in conflict: in the former, sea breakers strike rock in juxtaposed masses of light and dark, liquid and solid, volatile and immutable; while in the latter, two predatory types are locked in their respective flights for survival. One of his most compelling achievements, *The Fox Hunt* pits a red fox in deep snow against the

12 For example *The Two Guides,* 1876 (Sterling and Francine Clark Art Institute, Williamstown, Mass.); *The Herring Net,* 1885 (Art Institute of Chicago); *The Life Line,* 1884 (Philadelphia Museum of Art); *Undertow,* 1885 (Sterling and Francine Clark Art Institute, Williamstown, Mass.).

13 For example, *Winter Coast,* 1890 (Johnson Collection, Philadelphia Museum of Art), and *Gulf Stream,* 1899 (Metropolitan Museum of Art, New York).

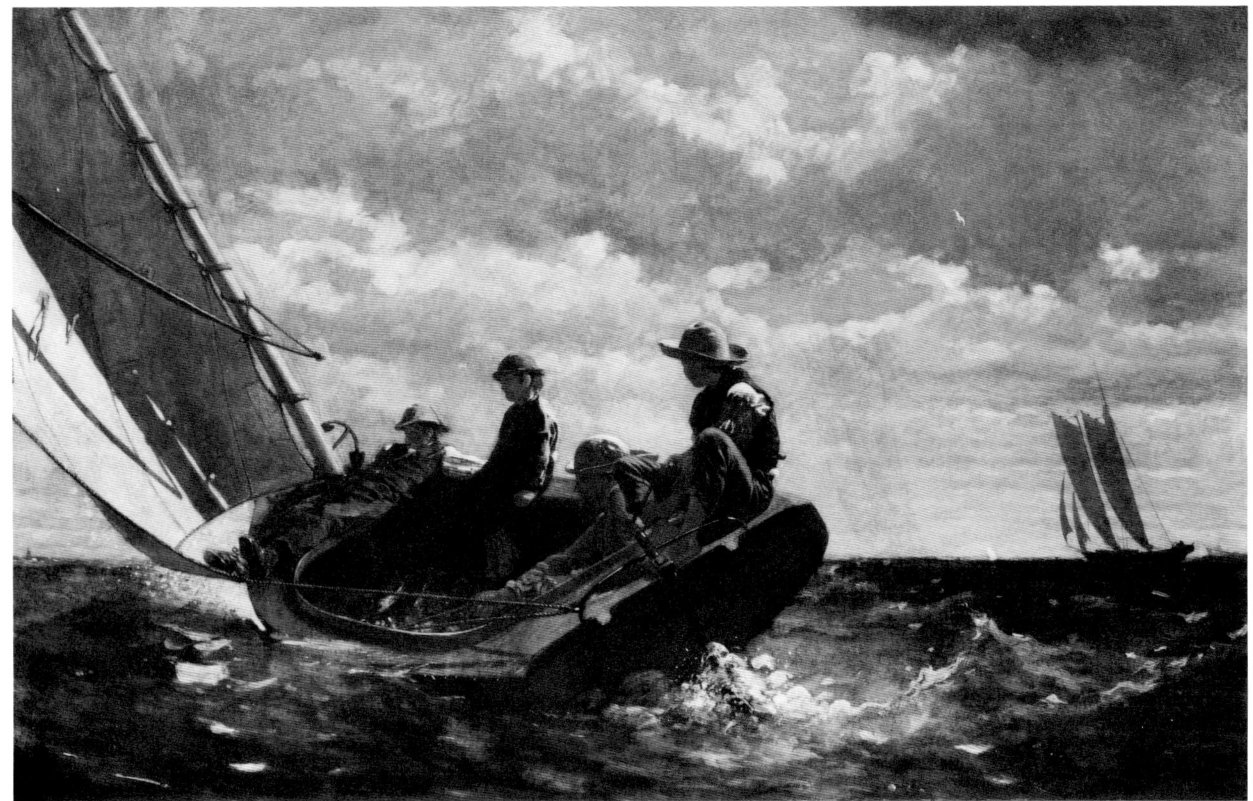

Fig. 3. Winslow Homer, Breezing Up, *1876. Oil on canvas. National Gallery of Art, Washington, D.C.; Gift of W. L. and May T. Mellon Foundation 1943*

parallel diagonal of two looming crows, fused into a single shape above. Altogether, the monochromatic power of this painting, the sharply incised silhouettes of animal and birds, and the fusion of beauty with violence form an important precedent for *Right and Left* a decade and a half later.

In a related process of pairings significant figures give way to significant masses, as in *Waiting for Dad* (1873; Collection of Mr. and Mrs. Paul Mellon) and *Breezing Up* (fig. 3). In the latter, Homer carefully set off the diagonal mass of a catboat in the left foreground with a large schooner on a parallel course in the right distance. The preliminary watercolor had included the tip of Eastern Point and the Gloucester harbor lighthouse; by removing reference to land and substituting another sailing vessel in his oil, Homer at once generalized, animated, and unified his theme.[14]

We may summarize these elements in Homer's stylistic evolution, as it leads up to his culminating image, by looking more fully at *Gloucester Farm* (fig. 4), a thoroughly characteristic work dating from the center of his career. Here we have two young farm hands, a boy and girl standing statuesquely alone in the foreground of a sloping farmyard. From their still, columnar stance and our rather low vantage point looking up the hill, we tend to see them as taller, more contemplative, and perhaps more adult than they are. Besides their crossing glances, and the obvious contrast of male and female, we also note the familiar repetition of other forms behind in the pair of cows at the upper left and two barn structures at the upper right.

[14] Homer continued with expressive and simplified paired shapes in *Eight Bells*, 1886 (Addison Gallery, Andover, Mass.). Even bolder was his composition a decade later of *The Lookout—"All's Well"* (Museum of Fine Arts, Boston); here he virtually filled his canvas with the two large forms of the fisherman's head and ship's bell behind. This juxtaposition is, of course, both one of compared masses as well as sounds.

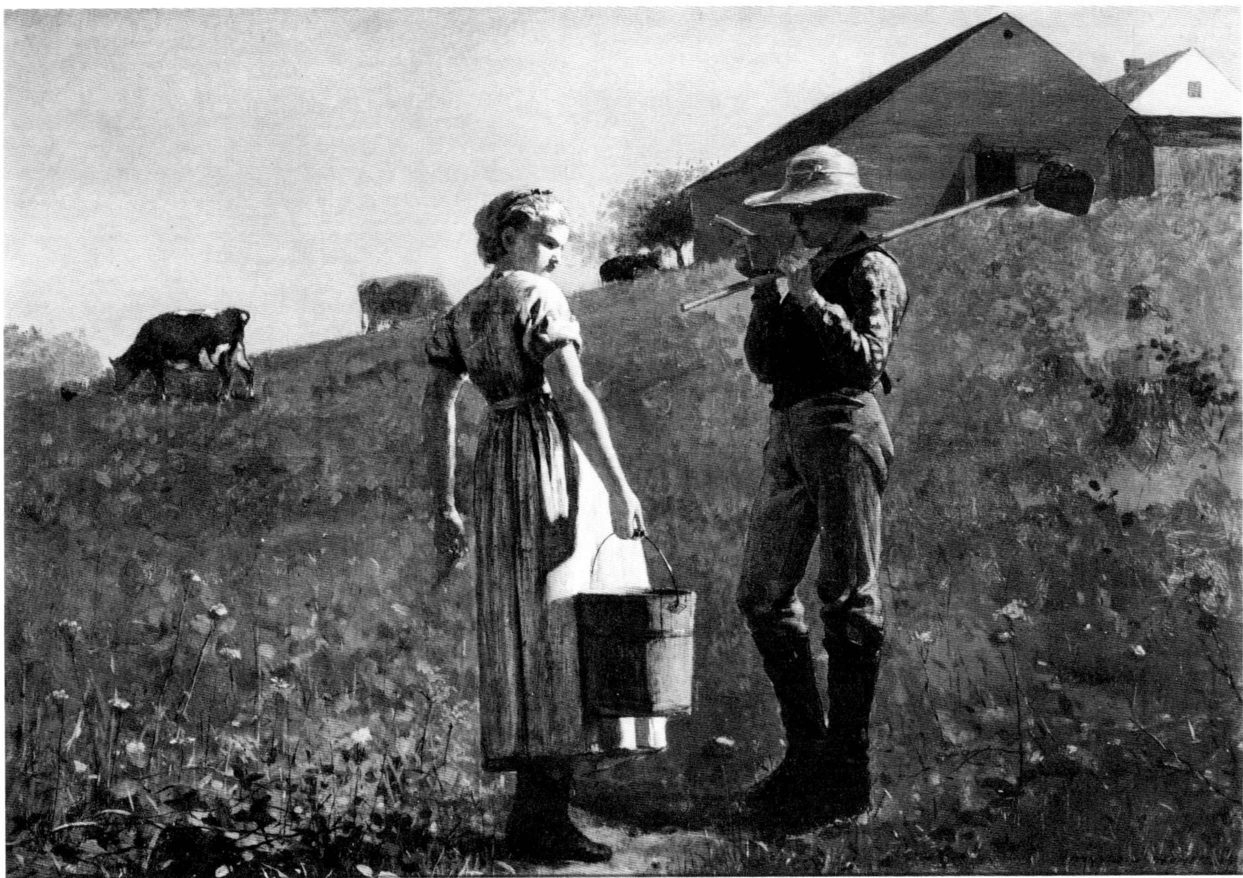

Fig. 4. Winslow Homer, Gloucester Farm, *1874. Oil on canvas. Philadelphia Museum of Art; Purchase: John H. McFadden, Jr., Fund*

Although a relatively colorful picture, Homer has kept himself to broad flat zones of almost unmodulated primary hues. The notably high horizon formed by the rising hillside helps to set off the strongly defined figures before us, a device made more radically expressive in *Right and Left.* Even in such a pastoral image as this there is a gravity of mood, largely deriving from Homer's calculated design and *yin-yang* subject matter (i.e., complementary opposites), which forecasts the charged vision he was to give many years later to a mere brace of golden-eye ducks.

In the imagery of hunting especially Homer was able to fuse into one whole two parallel and interconnected levels of experience: his personal love of wilderness sporting adventure and his artistic investigation of nature's universal forces. Throughout his mature career he had regularly depicted scenes, based on first-hand knowledge, of bird hunting and fishing. For the most part these were narrative and descriptive paintings, encapsulating familiar incidents in the pursuit of game and filled with local details of color and texture. At the same time he increasingly began to examine the mysterious and inexplicable moments of life and death caught in the balance, whether involving the hunter or hunted. During the decade of the nineties particularly we find this interesting interplay between commonplace observation and serious allusion. Also, probably due to his recent taking

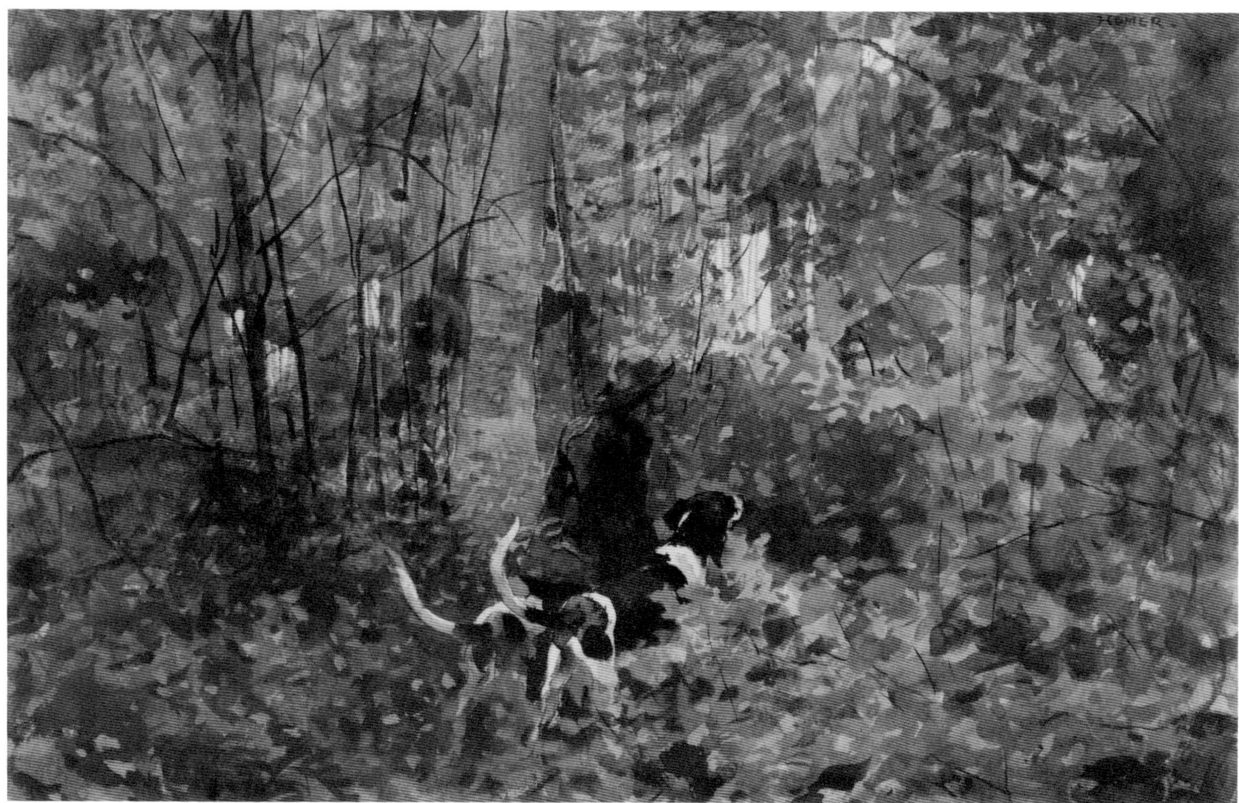

Fig. 5. Winslow Homer, On the Trail, *1892. Watercolor. National Gallery of Art, Washington, D.C.; Gift of Ruth K. Henschel in memory of her husband Charles R. Henschel*

up of photography, Homer's watercolors achieve a new boldness in juxtaposition of forms, as well as of scale and spatial relationships. A glance at a few paintings from this period will illustrate Homer's probing of both iconographical and formal possibilities.

The watercolor *On the Trail* (fig. 5), painted in 1892, shows a hunter with his two dogs pursuing some unseen game in dense woods. Although the myriad shapes and textures of the colorful foliage are brilliantly executed and our attention is focused on the highlighted central figures, the record of a huntsman's pursuit is a relatively conventional and straightforward genre image. Homer here associates the viewer with the position of the hunting man and hounds, while the game remains obscured somewhere in the distance. This relationship, of course, becomes dramatically reversed in *Right and Left*.

From the same year as *On the Trail* date Homer's watercolor and oil versions of *Hound and Hunter* (fig. 6), both giving us another confrontation between man and animal. Here in a dark corner of the woods at stream's edge (where a series of Homer watercolors also documented a deer coming to the water for a drink and then falling to a marksman's rifle), a youth attempts to secure a deer to his drifting canoe. He glances with some unease at his dog swimming back from midstream, and from this anxious face we become conscious of this vignette's several uncertainties. Is the deer actually dead, and a sinking weight under water to be lashed to the canoe before the dog

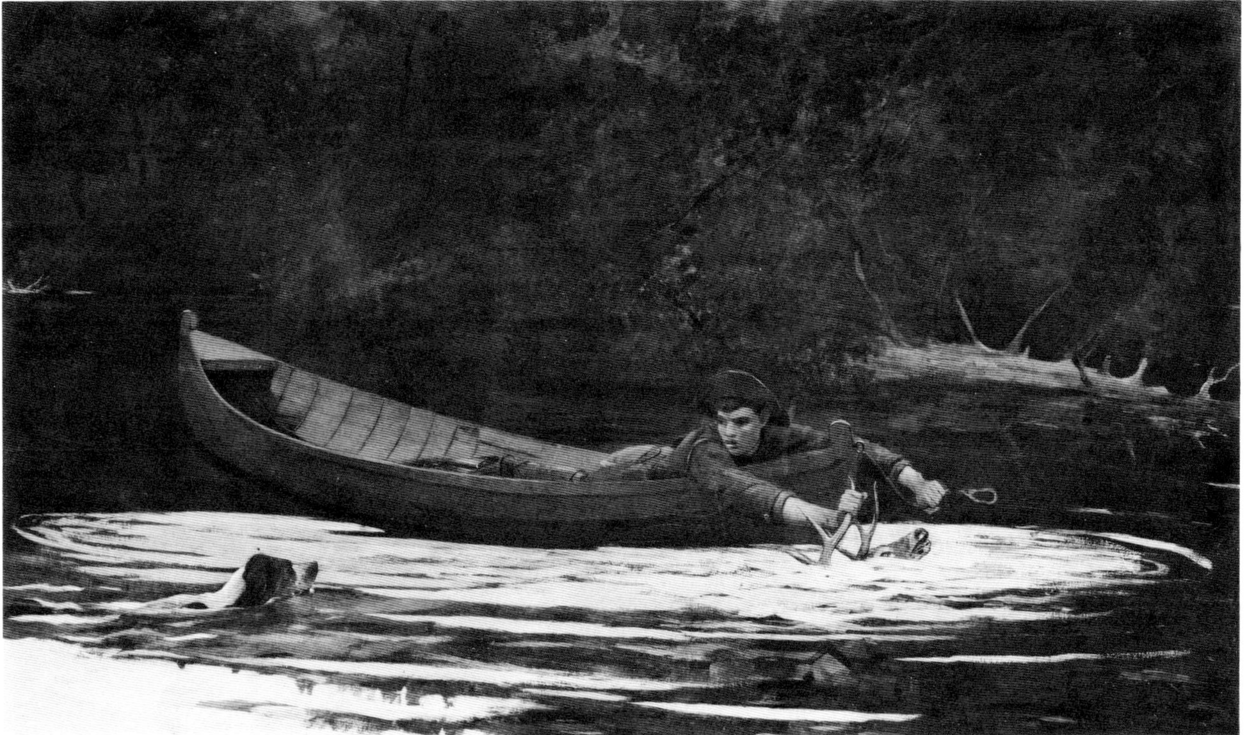

Fig. 6. Winslow Homer, Hound and Hunter, *1892. Oil on canvas. National Gallery of Art, Washington, D.C.; Gift of Stephen C. Clark 1947*

draws too close and interferes? The youth's rifle rests across the central thwart, presumably just used; but what of the bright eye of the deer just above water, still gleaming as if with life? In this darkly painted and closed environment humble and anonymous death acquires a mysterious, momentary grandeur.

The fishing watercolors of the nineties dealt with similar contests in one of Homer's most prolific and accomplished series, resulting from his regular visits to the Adirondacks woods and the inland waters of Quebec Province. Now for the first time he situates the hunted game—in this case trout leaping from Lake St. John and the Saguenay River (figs. 7 and 8)—pressed against the center foreground. By so doing Homer gives the fish an exaggerated scale comparable to the canoe and men behind, a dislocation attenuated to the extreme in *Right and Left.* In the later watercolor of 1897 the leaping trout also rises to cross the distant canoe, establishing a surprising intersection of near and far forms equally prophetic of the row boat locked momentarily behind the rising duck's feet in the later oil.

Ouananiche Fishing, Lake St. John retains a relatively conventional legibility of spatial recession from foreground to distant hillside and sky. By comparison, in *A Good Pool, Saguenay River* of 1895, Homer at once compressed and abstracted the pictorial space. Not only is the leaping trout much larger in contrast to canoe behind, but it is now sharply silhouetted against a flattened curtain of spray

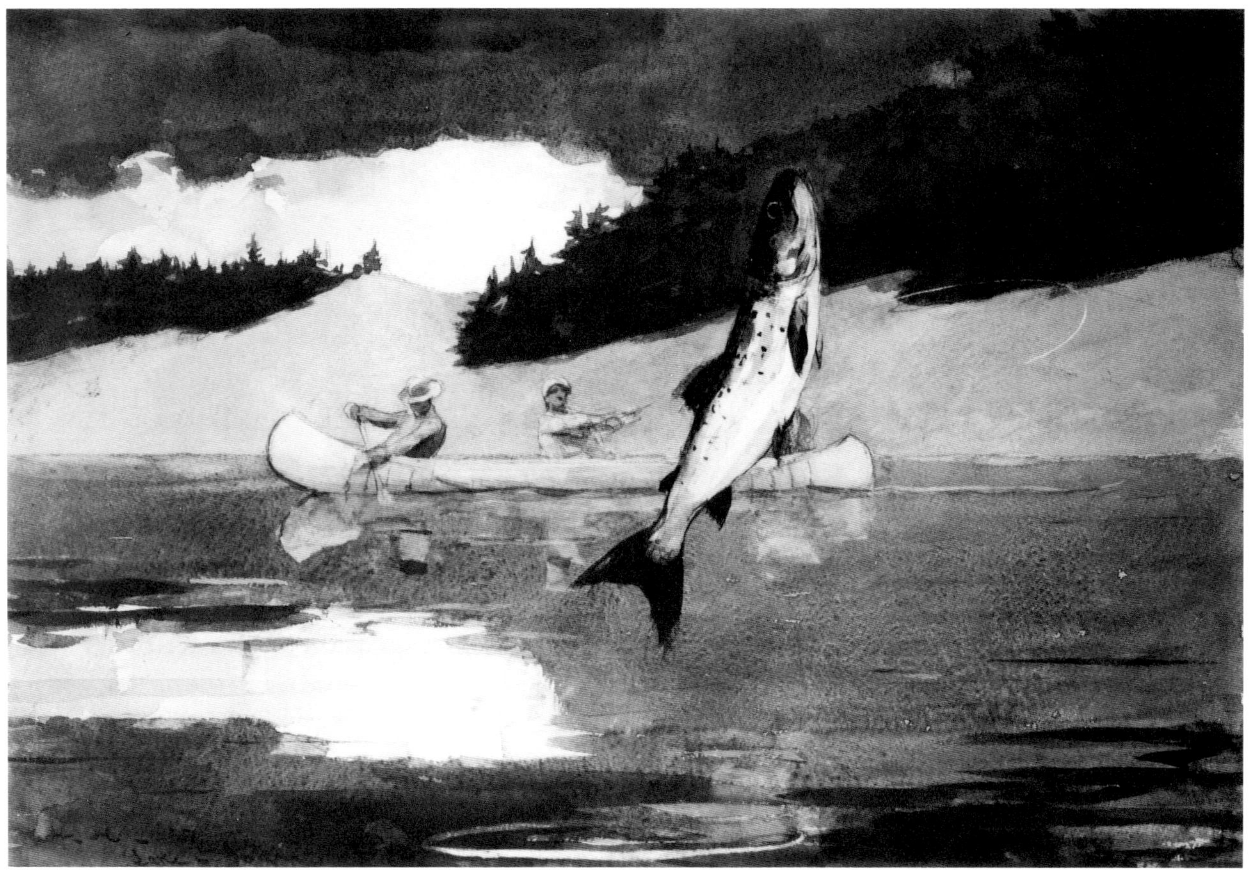

Fig. 7. Winslow Homer, Ouananiche Fishing, Lake St. John, Quebec, *1897. Watercolor. Courtesy, Museum of Fine Arts, Boston; William Wilkins Warren Fund*

and sky. Anticipating *Right and Left,* its horizon and view into depth are obscured. To some extent the sharp freezing of spontaneous action, as well as the two-dimensional compression of forms, must owe something to Homer's taking his own photographs on these trips. In any case, the result is a subtle transformation of landscape subject matter into quasi-still life. Indeed, about the same time Homer painted *Two Trout* (IBM Corporation, New York) showing gaffed fish hanging against a flat abstracted background of wall.[15] This watercolor of 1889 is as close to pure still life as he would come. More pertinent here are the several inventive variations he made in subsequent years, such as *Fish and Butterflies,* (1900; Sterling and Francine Clark Art Institute, Williamstown, Massachusetts), in which the three colorful shapes hang suspended against an impenetrable screen of dark water. These tightly framed landscapes thus approach the intimacy and immobility of a still life. As such, they invite us to contemplate both their formal purity and their lifting of humble sentiment into heroic isolation.

On one level we may understand this heightened imaginativeness of design and meaning in Homer's late art as the fruition of creative imperatives generated throughout his career. Another way to appreciate the freshness, and modernism, of this vision is to reflect on his pictorial constructs at the turn of the century in the larger context

[15] For a discussion of Homer's fish still life in the context of other late-nineteenth-century paintings of similar subjects, see William H. Gerdts and Russell Burke, *American Still-Life Painting* (New York, 1971), chap. 9: "Fish and Game Still Life," 121-132.

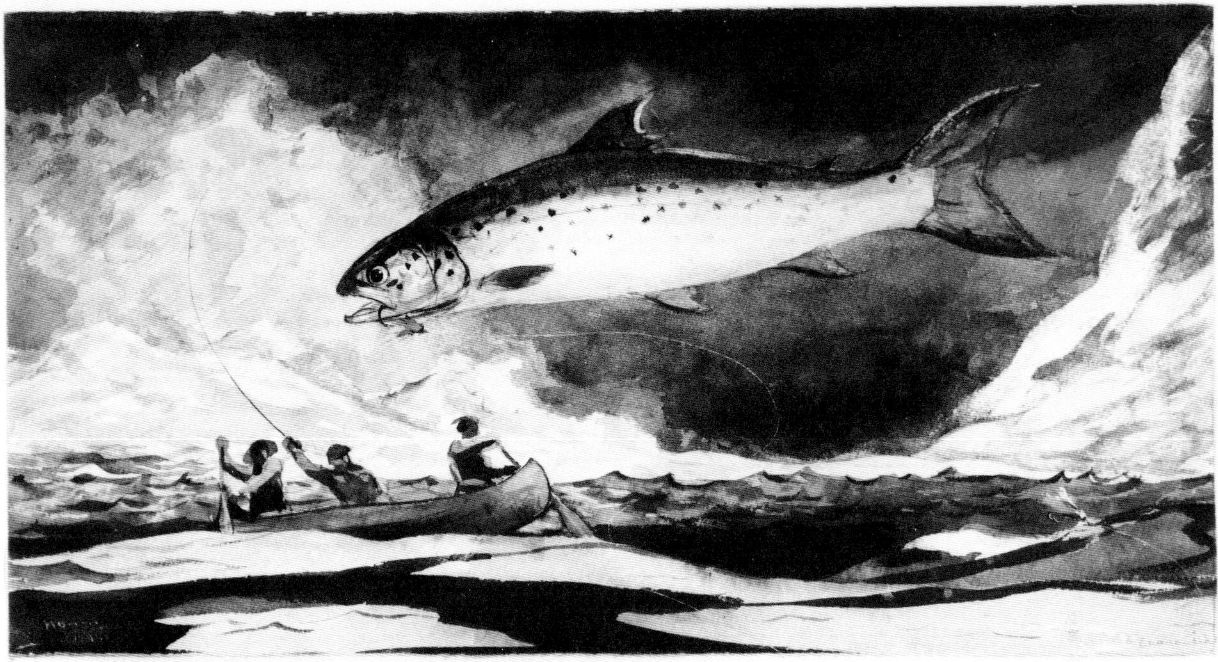

Fig. 8. Winslow Homer, A Good Pool, Saguenay River, *1895. Watercolor over pencil on paper. Sterling and Francine Clark Art Institute, Williamstown, Massachusetts*

of contemporary Western art. During the decade and a half between *A Good Pool, Saguenay River* and *Right and Left,* for example, Claude Monet was concurrently pursuing in his great water lily series a similar abstraction of space. *Les Nympheas* of 1905 (fig. 9) is characteristic in the way he appears to bring together the surface of water with that of the picture plane. Whether we read this as a looking down closely onto the pond's reflections, or a lifting up of the watery plane until the upper horizon disappears, the result is a cropping of any measured or measurable view into traditional depth. The bright patches of water lilies float both literally in nature and figuratively on canvas. Homer's contracting of spatial recession in his fishing watercolors and the ambiguity of environment surrounding the birds in *Right and Left* serve to remind how, more than just chronologically, his mature vision partook of twentieth-century art.

Thus, we have seen how Homer's last paintings conclude a long, steady evolution of formal and iconographic concerns, which derive at once from his own vision as well as from a wider contemporary context. It is now worth summarizing this development in his specific imagery of birds. A good starting point, and early benchmark by which to measure the creative distance traveled in *Right and Left,* is his 1869 canvas, *Rocky Coast and Gulls* (fig. 10). Dating from just after Homer's return from Paris, this painting is curiously perfunctory and innovative at the same time. While its bright colors and fresh handling of paint reflect his recent awareness of early French impressionism, it is a view of unfocused visual interest. On the whole it is an ordinary description of landscape, with the incidental narrative details of four gulls feeding in the foreground. The spatial

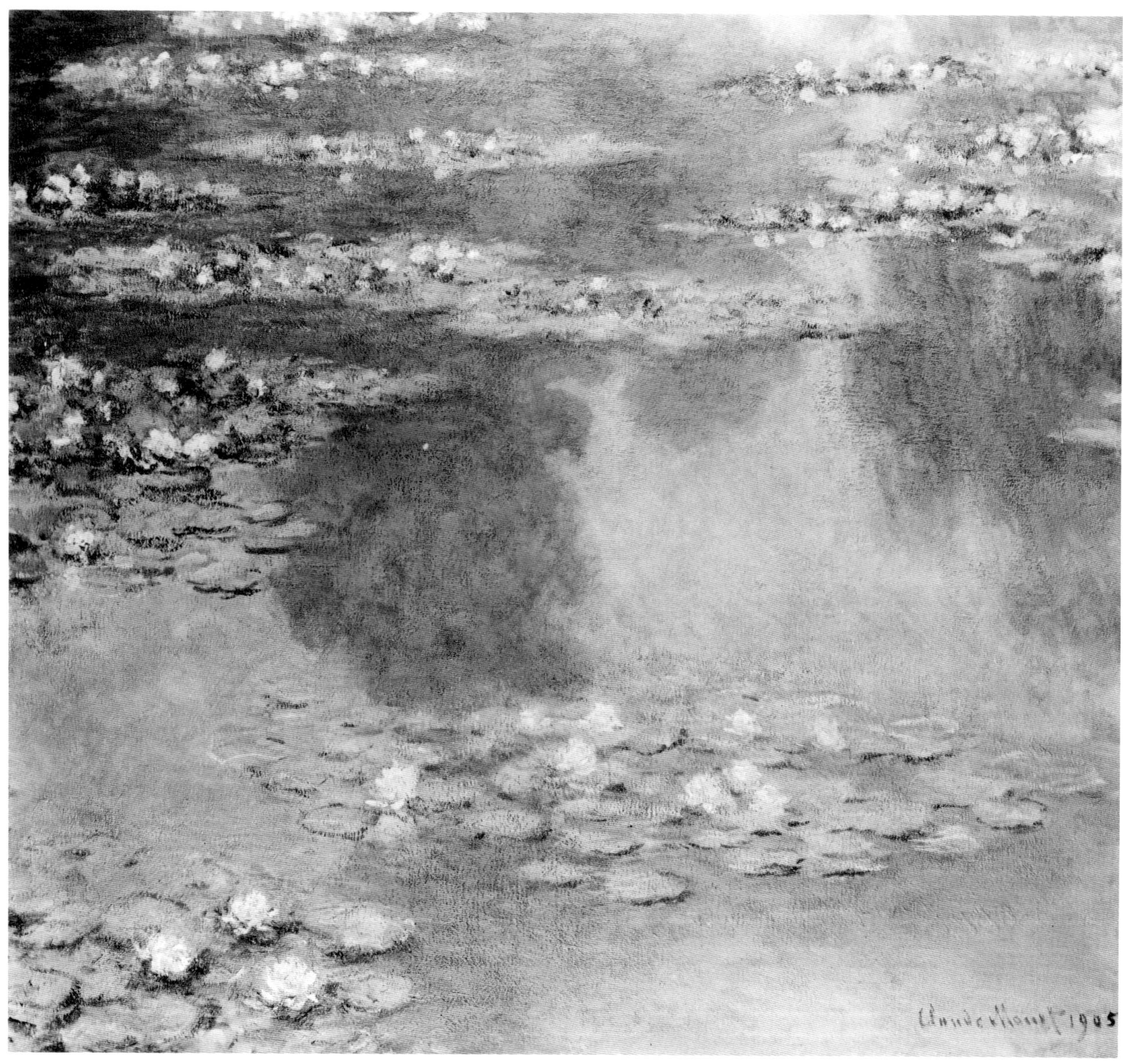

Fig. 9. Claude Monet, Les Nympheas, *1905. Oil on canvas. Museum of Fine Arts, Boston; Bequest of Alexander Cochrane*

recession is also relatively conventional, our eyes being carried from the white birds to the spray in the middle ground and on to the dots of sailboats on the horizon. Yet just as our glance moves back into space, it seems also to rise upward across the flattened and almost unobstructed planes of beach, rocks, water, and sky. For all its implication of depth, this unusually high horizon and cropped sky have the effect of compacting the pictorial space. A similar strip of bright sky runs across the upper edge of *Right and Left,* though now it is spatially ambiguous and indeterminate, forcing our attention back to the foreground plane. Here we and the ducks are uncomfortably locked into place.

As Homer's interest and pleasure in hunting grew during his later years at Prout's Neck, he turned more frequently to his sporting

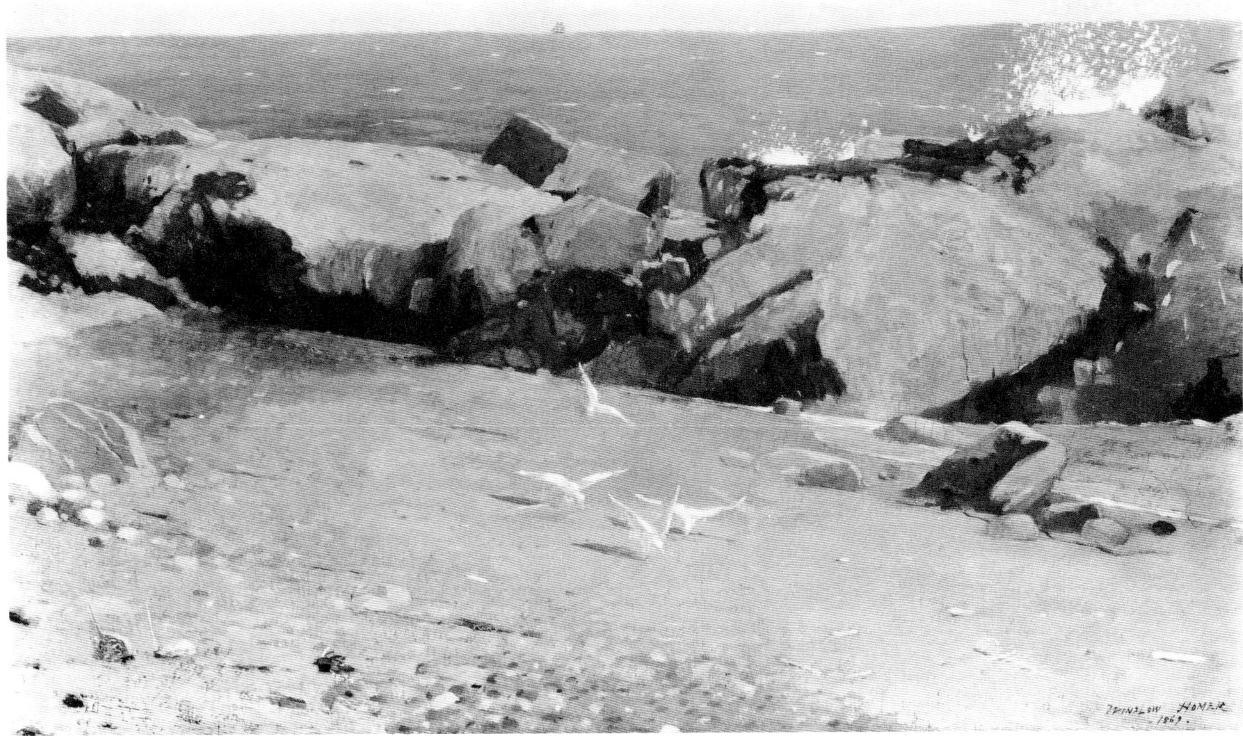

Fig. 10. Winslow Homer, Rocky Coast and Gulls, *1869. Oil on canvas. Museum of Fine Arts, Boston; Bequest of Grenville H. Norcross*

experiences for pictorial subject matter. About 1896 he drew *Wild Goose in Flight* in preparation for a large oil he completed the following year (figs. 11 and 12). The strong drawing in black and white crayon is interesting for both its foreshortening and its emphatic linear outlining of the bird in flight. Although it clearly relates to the three airborne birds in *Wild Geese,* the drawing matches none of them exactly. Beneath the goose in the drawing are two cursory notations of form cut off at the bottom edge of the page. We can read these variously as suggestions of beach grasses, which will mark the ragged dunes in the oil; or as closeup studies of a goose's webbed feet, plunging downward as they will not in this oil but in *Right and Left;* or, as tongues of spray rising from wave crests, also to appear beneath the ducks in the later painting. In any case, it is evident that Homer sought to capture a powerfully expressive contour of his bird in flight, achieved both by the simplified outline and the tension of a foreshortened torso straining in motion.

The painting of *Wild Geese* employs that now-familiar low vantage point and high horizon line. Significantly, it gives us a sequence of actions: three geese rising from the bushes and two fallen at our feet. Like Eadweard Muybridge's photograph of birds in motion (fig. 17), the three upper geese demonstrate the serial wing motions of a single bird lifting off the ground. This notion of a sequential action is of course another important element intensified in Homer's later ducks under fire. It remains uncertain in *Wild Geese* whether the birds in the foreground have fallen there from a hunter's shot or from flying into a nearby lighthouse.[16] But their inert forms in death

[16] Citing Downes, Beam notes that this painting was originally titled *At the Foot of the Lighthouse.* See Beam, *Homer,* 248.

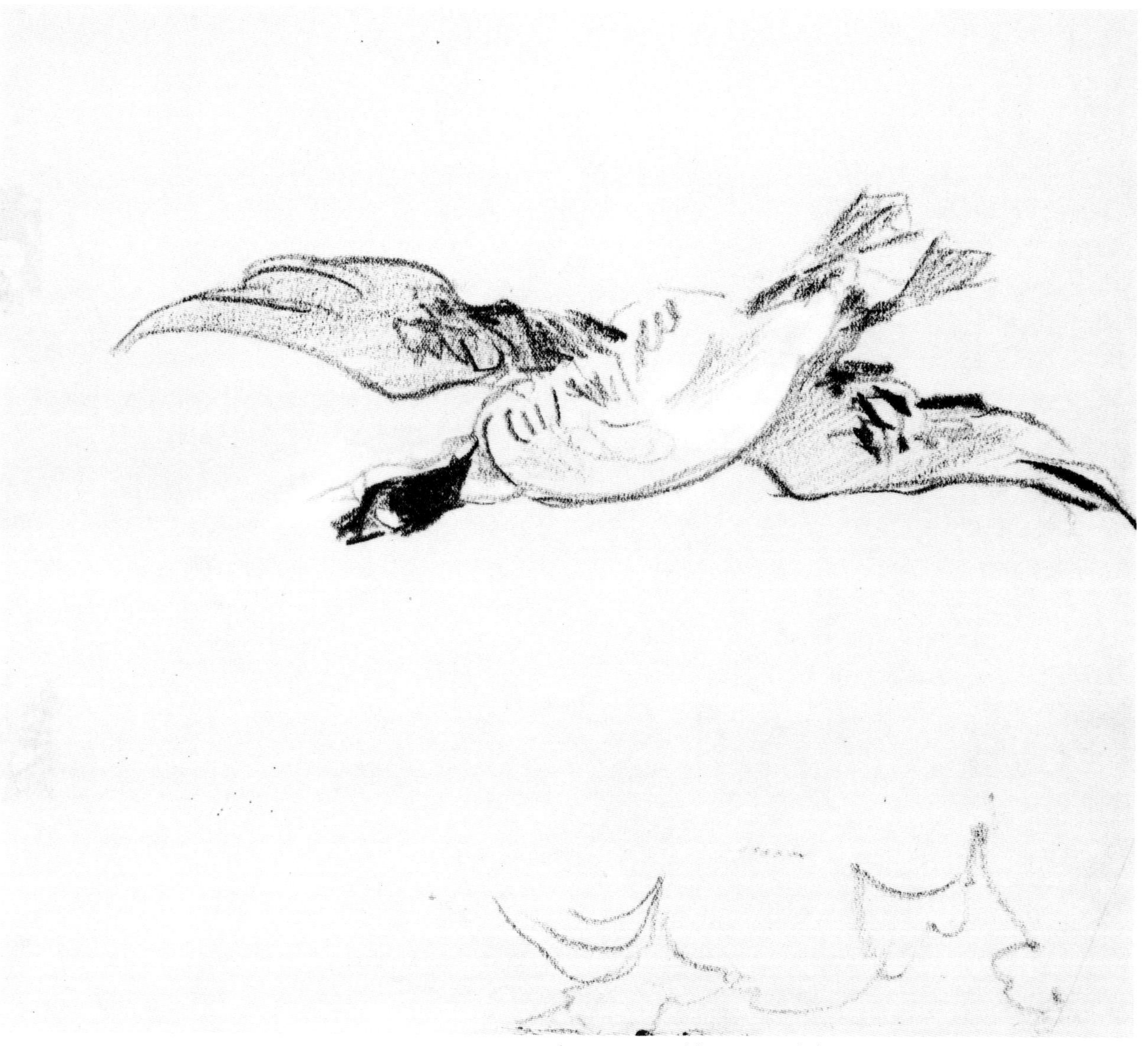

Fig. 11. Winslow Homer, Wild Goose in Flight, *c. 1896. Drawing. Cooper-Hewitt Museum, The Smithsonian Institution's National Museum of Design. Photograph: Scott Hyde, New York*

establish a characteristic polar contrast to their vital counterparts flying above. *Right and Left* distills this contrast further, to a point of mysterious intensity. Even more, such *yin-yang* interlocking of the bright and active with the dark and passive—first seen in the explicitly masculine-feminine interplay of *The Life Line* (1884; Philadelphia Museum of Art), *Undertow* (1885; Sterling and Francine Clark Art Institute, Williamstown, Massachusetts), and *Gloucester Farm*—seems to approach the intentional artificiality of a still-life arrangement, yet another compositional decision reemployed a decade later.

If all the foregoing constitutes the cumulative imagery leading Homer to his last great work, there remains for our consideration the external world of art which in varying degrees appears to have

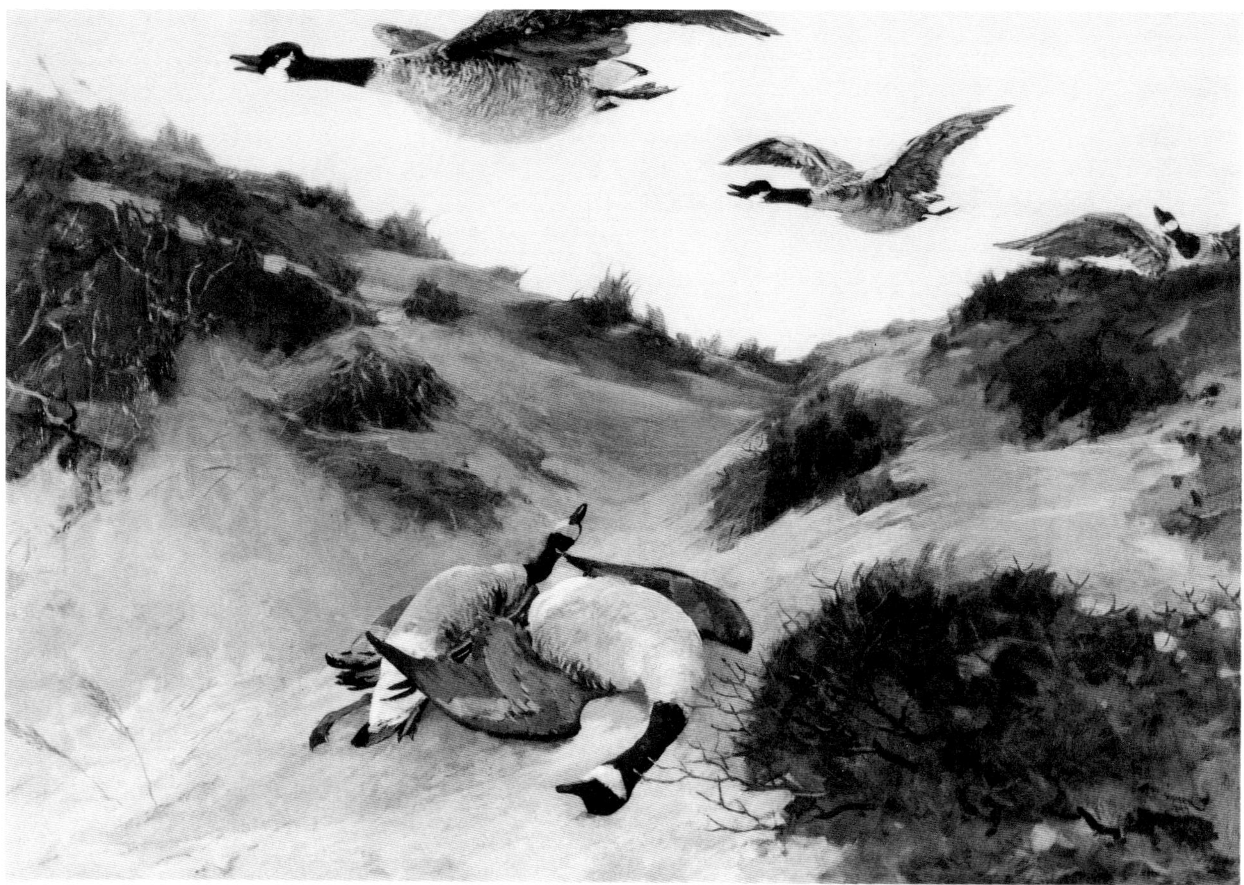

Fig. 12. Winslow Homer, Wild Geese, *1897. Oil on Canvas. Collection of Charles Shipman Payson, promised gift to the Portland Museum of Art.*

contributed its own shaping forces to his "most surprising picture." During the last quarter of the nineteenth century, for example, several of Homer's contemporaries were painting highly personal still lifes of birds in isolation. While there is no evidence that Homer directly knew of their work, such images as Albert Ryder's *Dead Bird* and Alexander Pope's *Trumpeter Swan* (figs. 13 and 14) indicate a shared pictorial language. A native of New Bedford, Massachusetts, Ryder began painting in the 1870s simplified scenes of the local landscape, often with a horse or cow alone in the quiet glow of evening light. *Dead Bird* is thought to date from this period of relatively naturalist subjects, though its haunting meditative aura and abstracted treatment also hint of the deeply mystical and hermetic visions he was to paint in subsequent years. Especially relevant here to our comparison with Homer's *Right and Left* is the virtually monochromatic palette (of dark yellow for the bird and sandy brown for the textured ground) of *Dead Bird;* its theme of pathetic vulnerability in the animal world; and the flattening of the bird against a spatially ambiguous background. More speculative is the question of the extent to which this fragile creature is to be associated with Ryder's own brooding personality, just as we may wonder if Homer's scene of surprising confrontation might reveal some inexplicable animus bursting from reclusion at the close of his career.

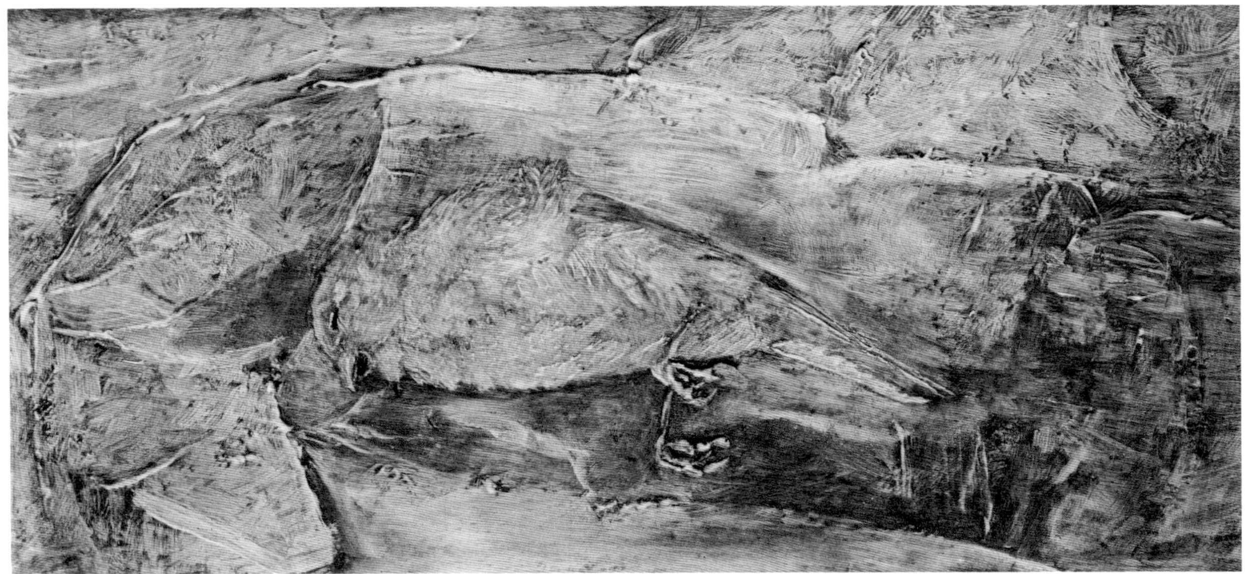

Fig. 13. Albert Pinkham Ryder, Dead Bird, *before 1880. Oil on wood panel. The Phillips Collection, Washington, D.C.*

Like Homer, Pope cared deeply about the natural world, primarily as a conservationist. This led him to paint a series of animal trophy illusions, with the dead game beautifully hung against wooden doors or boards. An earlier version of *The Trumpeter Swan,* dated 1900, for many years belonged to the Massachusetts Society for the Preservation of Cruelty to Animals; presumably it was undertaken to call attention to the impending extinction of that exquisite species.[17] In the 1900 oil (Fine Arts Museums of San Francisco) the great bird hangs alone against a finely paneled door, while in the second version eleven years later Pope added vines of ivy and a hanging shotgun. These references to nature and man add new visual interest to the composition while retaining the spare two-dimensional design of the earlier work. Again, the calculated still-life arrangement against a partially abstracted background parallels Homer's *Right and Left,* as obviously does the juxtaposition of bird and gun. But Homer's transcending achievement is that *Right and Left* remains as much landscape as still life, and as such compells a more provocative human involvement.

[17] See Alfred Frankenstein, *The Reality of Appearance: The Trompe L'Oeil Tradition in American Painting,* exh. cat., University Art Museum (Berkeley, Calif., 1970), 134; and Gerdts and Burke, *American Still-Life Painting,* 156.

Scholars simply do not have the evidence, beyond a few pieces of information, to know what works by other artists Homer knew first hand. There is accumulating documentation about his respective visits to France in 1867 and England in 1881-1882 to indicate some awareness by Homer of Barbizon art, oriental decorative arts, and English painting, prints, and photography. Even before his trip to England Homer appears to have gained some familiarity with mid-nineteenth-century English art through his work as an illustrator in Boston. During the 1860s and seventies several art magazines carried reproductions of drawings by Edwin Landseer and a number of the Pre-Raphaelites, who strongly influenced illustrators working on both sides of the Atlantic. An especially intriguing possibility is that Homer at some point may have seen Landseer's work in particular,

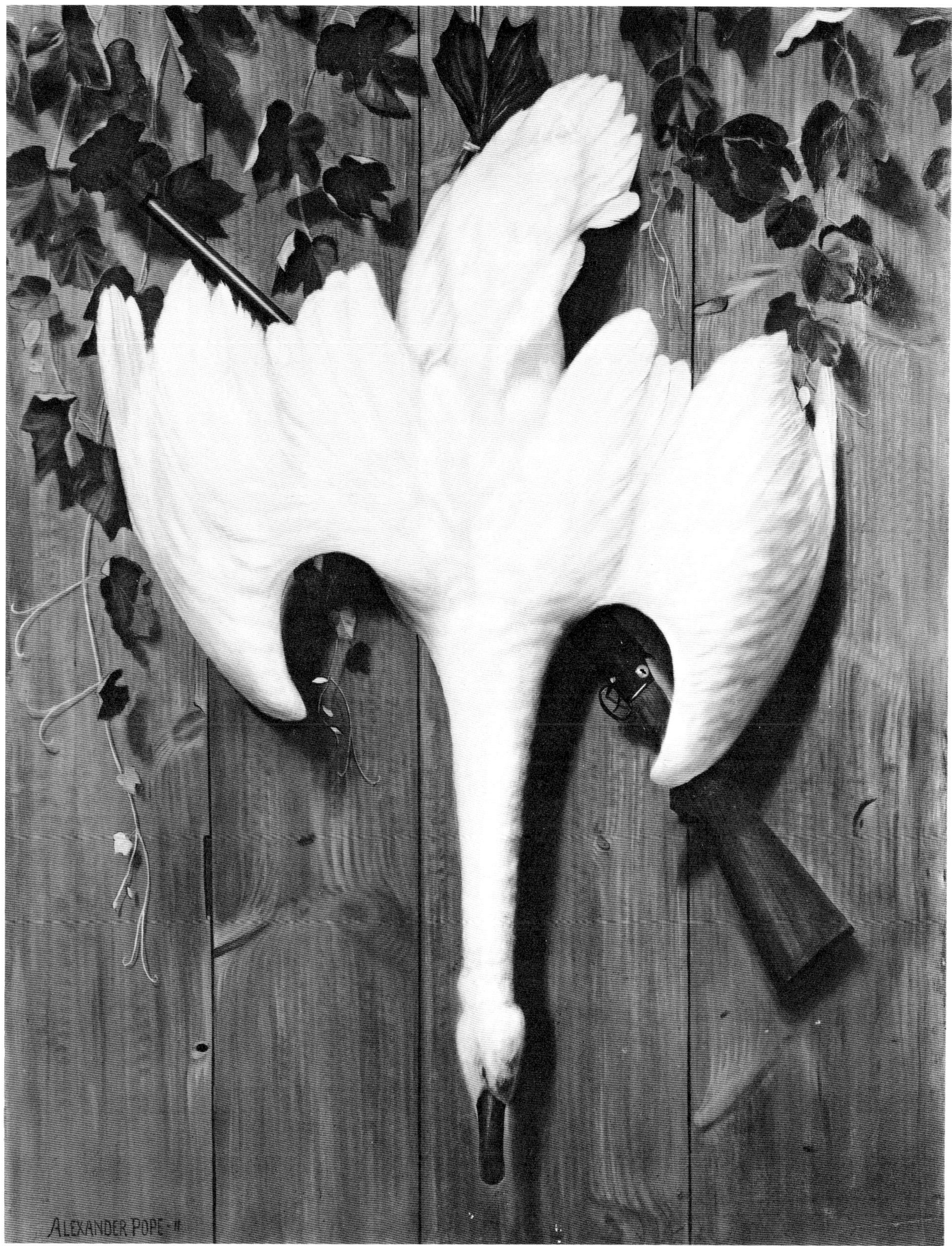

Fig. 14. Alexander Pope, The Trumpeter Swan, *1911. Oil on canvas. Private collection. Photograph: Helga Photo Studio, New York*

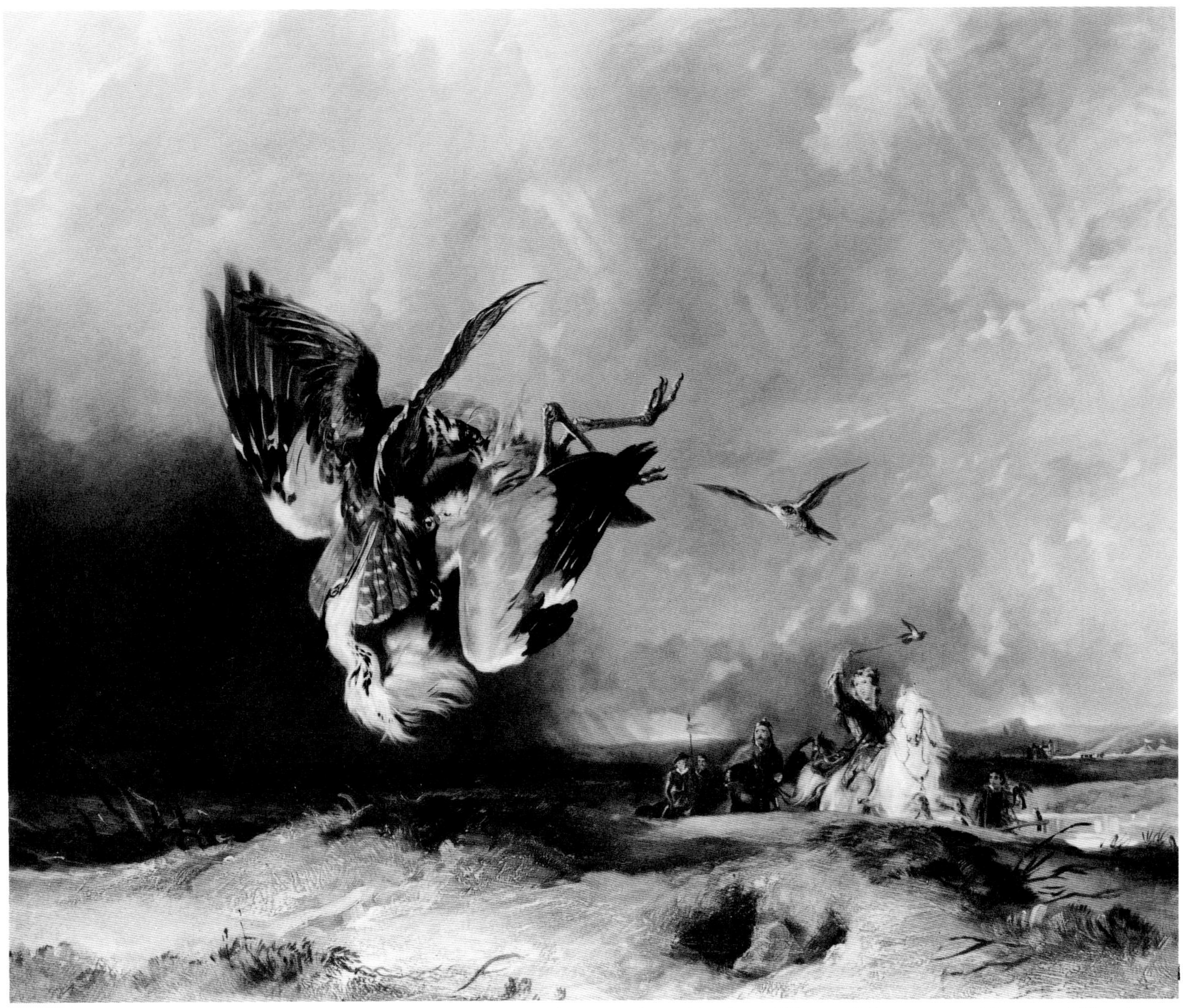

Fig. 15. Edwin Landseer, Hawk and Heron. *Oil on canvas. Museum of Fine Arts, Springfield, Massachusetts, The James Philip Gray Collection*

for *Hawk and Heron Hunt* (fig. 15) by the English painter suggests a surprising correlation with *Right and Left.* Not only do we have here an image with the hunters in the background, but the two powerful birds are locked in mortal combat, silhouetted strongly before us, and our vantage point is partially elevated to place the viewer close to this aerial drama.[18]

Among the few surviving items from his library, we know Homer owned and frequently consulted an English translation of M. E. Chevreul's *Laws of Contrast of Colour.*[19] More generally, all of Homer's biographers have discussed the painter's friendship with John La Farge, and through him Homer's exposure to Japanese prints. Albert Gardner reminds us that such prints were brought into the United States as early as 1855, and that La Farge often conversed about them in New York at the Studio Building, where Homer for a time was also to work.[20] Beam notes that La Farge was the one artist with whom Homer enjoyed talking about the practice and theory of art, and that La Farge had brought back his own orientalizing

[18] See Albert Ten Eyck Gardner, *Winslow Homer, American Artist: His World and His Work* (New York, 1961), chap. 4, "Homer in Paris—1867," 89-118; John Wilmerding, *Winslow Homer* (New York, 1972), chap. 2, "Painting What is Seen and Known," 41-83, and chap. 4, "A Stern Poetry of Feeling," 131-163; Wilmerding, "Winslow Homer's English Period," *The American Art Journal,* 7 no. 2 (Nov. 1975): 60-69; and William H. Gerdts, "Winslow Homer in Cullercoats," *Yale University Art Gallery Bulletin,* 36, no. 2 (Spring 1977): 18-35. With specific regard to the Landseer parallel, see Gardner, *Homer,* 156. I am grateful to Peter Sutton for bringing this possible connection to my attention.

[19] M. E. Chevreul, *The Laws of Contrast of Colour* (London, 1859). See David Tatham, "Winslow Homer's Library," *The American Art Journal,* 9, no. 1 (May 1977): 92-98.

[20] Gardner, *Homer,* 96.

watercolors from his trip with Henry Adams in 1886 to Japan and the South Seas.[21]

Homer himself had certainly seen oriental paintings or prints during his Paris trip, when he visited the great international exposition there. In the next few years he executed several illustrations for *Harper's* that were clearly adapted from Japanese graphics.[22] The Japanese influence was pervasive in later nineteenth-century American and European art, as we well know from the work of James Whistler and Mary Cassatt. Among the most popular graphics were the colorful prints of Hokusai and Hiroshige, and several authors have convincingly suggested the influence of the former's *Mt. Fuji* series on such compositions by Homer as *Guide Carrying Deer* (1891; Portland Museum of Art, Maine), and *Kissing the Moon* (1904; Addison Gallery, Andover, Massachusetts).[23]

Since we do not know which specific Japanese prints or screens Homer could have seen in Boston, New York, or elsewhere on his travels, it is worth citing just a couple of the most characteristic and accessible examples. Hiroshige's *Eagle Swooping down from the Sky,* 1857 (fig. 16), from his series Famous Views of Edo, is typical of the numerous woodblock engravings he executed featuring various birds in landscape settings. Giving particular attention to the colorful plumage and distinctive silhouettes of each species, Hiroshige often set his birds in dramatic contrast to flat expanses of open sky or earth. Here in fact we have the startling shape of the eagle's arcing wings fixed in visual tension with the earth receding far away below. This device of a boldly patterned form in the foreground set directly against space is precisely what Homer so effectively employs in *Right and Left.* More intriguing is whether Homer could have seen Maruyama Okyo's large painted screen *Geese Flying over a Beach* (fig. 17). Charles L. Freer acquired this in 1897 (incidentally the year Homer painted his oil of that subject, fig. 12), and although he maintained most of his collection in Detroit, he did lend this screen occasionally for viewing in New York and other places on the east coast.[24] Certainly, its cunning contrast of the two birds in flight and the evocatively open space are fully appropriate in spirit to Homer's last bird painting.

Within the history of the graphic arts in America there are two potential sources it is tempting to associate with Homer. The first is Eadweard Muybridge's monumental photographic series of stopped action photographs known as *Animal Locomotion: An Electro-Photographic Investigation of Consecutive Phases of Animal Movements.* This the noted photographer had begun in 1872, completed in 1885 and published two years later. The eleven folio volumes included nearly eight-hundred photo-engravings, devoted to documenting all manner of movements by men, women, children, horses, and other animals. Some two dozen prints in the final volume, *Wild Animals and Birds,* depict various birds at rest and in flight, including cranes, geese, and ducks. Because this sub-group constitutes a small proportion of the whole project, and the horse series in particular had attained a certain fame through the widely publicized commission for Leland Stanford, historians have infrequently examined the bird photographs.[25] Yet Muybridge's stopped-action frames of such birds as the cockatoo and eagle in

[21] Beam, *Homer,* 162, 191, 205.

[22] For example, *International Tea Party,* watercolor, 1868 (Cooper-Hewitt Museum, New York); *St. Valentine's Day* in *Harper's Weekly,* Feb. 22, 1868; and *The Chinese in New York—Scene in a Baxter Street Club House* in *Harper's Weekly,* Mar. 7, 1874.

[23] See Gardner, *Homer,* 206-207; Beam, *Homer,* 107-108; and Wilmerding, *Homer,* 171.

[24] Beam is one of the few to comment on this specific image as a possible source, *Homer,* 248. I also wish to acknowledge with gratitude the helpful assistance of Martin Amt of the Freer Gallery of Art.

[25] For example, the bird photographs are neither analyzed nor illustrated in Van Deren Coke, *The Painter and the Photograph, from Delacroix to Warhol* (Albuquerque, N.M., 1964); Kevin MacDonnell, *Eadweard Muybridge, The Man who invented the moving picture* (Boston, 1972); or *Eadweard Muybridge, The Stanford Years,* exh. cat., Stanford University Museum of Art (Stanford, Calif., 1972). Single illustrations without discussion of the subject appear in Aaron Scharf, *Art and Photography* (Baltimore, 1969), 169; and Gordon Hendricks, *Eadweard Muybridge, The Father of the Motion Picture* (New York, 1975), 169.

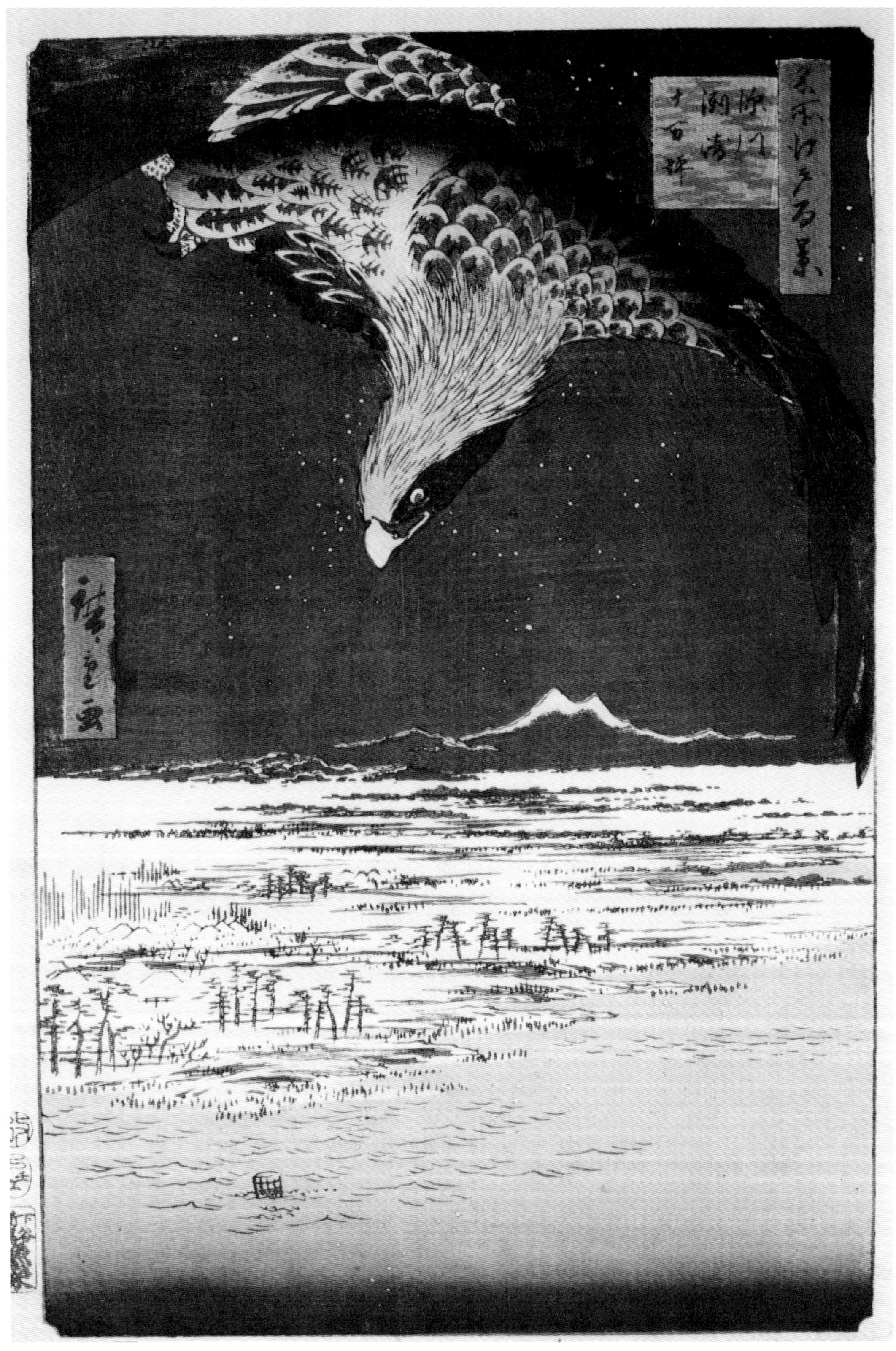

Fig. 16. Ichiryusai Hiroshige, An Eagle Swooping down from the Sky, *1857. Woodblock color print, from the series Meisho Edo Hyakkei ("Famous views of Edo"). Freer Gallery of Art, Washington, D.C.*

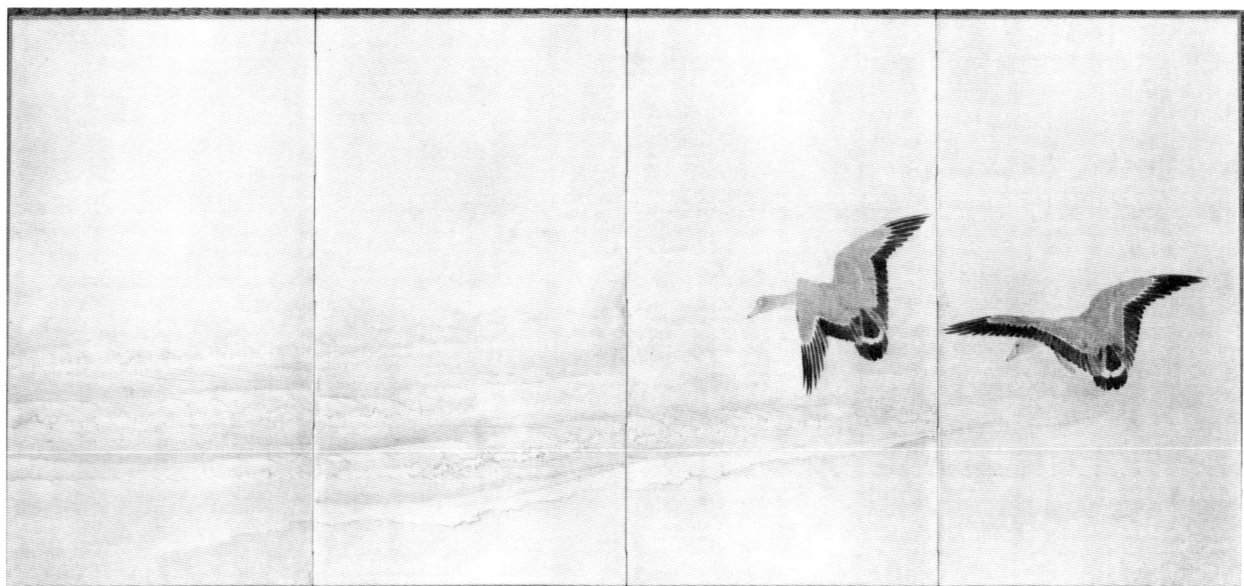

Fig. 17. Maruyama Okyo, Geese Flying over a Beach, *Edo period (18th. c.). Ink on paper. Freer Gallery of Art, Washington, D.C.*

flight (fig. 18) display striking patterns and profiles that suggest interesting correlations with Homer's ducks. And we should not forget that Homer himself, with a strong feeling for the graphic arts in his career, was in these same years taking his own photographs.

The second graphic precedent from the native tradition even more demonstrably close to *Right and Left* is John James Audubon's folio rendering of the *Golden-Eye Duck,* engraved in color by Robert Havell as plate CCCXLII in the ambitious four-volume *Birds of America* (fig. 19).[26] Attempting to record all the species he could find across North America, Audubon began supervision of his publication in 1827 and brought it to conclusion eleven years later, with a total of 435 plates documenting 497 species. The original watercolor is somewhat softer in handling than Havell's print, which shifts Audubon's blue sky more toward gray-green and hardens his fluid cloud layers to the scalloped design we see here. Obviously a set of the prints would have been far more available to Homer, and indeed the lower cloud edge in the engraving especially anticipates the lower cresting wave in his oil.

It was Audubon's achievement to combine an ornithologist's desire for accuracy of identifying detail with an artist's sensibility for pure, expressive form. His aim foremost was to capture the distinguishing physical characteristics of each species and, where possible, to intimate something of its habitat and behavior. Here he is interested in illustrating the subtle differences in plumage and size between the male on the left and female to the right. As Audubon noted, this bird was "equally fitted for travelling through the air and the water,"[27] and, appropriately, he shows one swooping downward, the other swiftly rising. Homer employs a similar contrast of motions, in reverse, though he is less concerned with the scientific marks of gender. More crucially, he removes his birds from the neutral and generic presentation of Audubon and gives them a vital,

[26] Samuel M. Green is the one historian who has cited this specific plate from Audubon as an inspiration for Homer's painting. See his *American Art* (New York, 1966), 403. The original watercolor is now in the collection of The New-York Historical Society.

[27] Quoted in Marshall B. Davidson, *The Original Water-Color Paintings by John James Audubon for "The Birds of America,"* (New York, 1966), pl. 248.

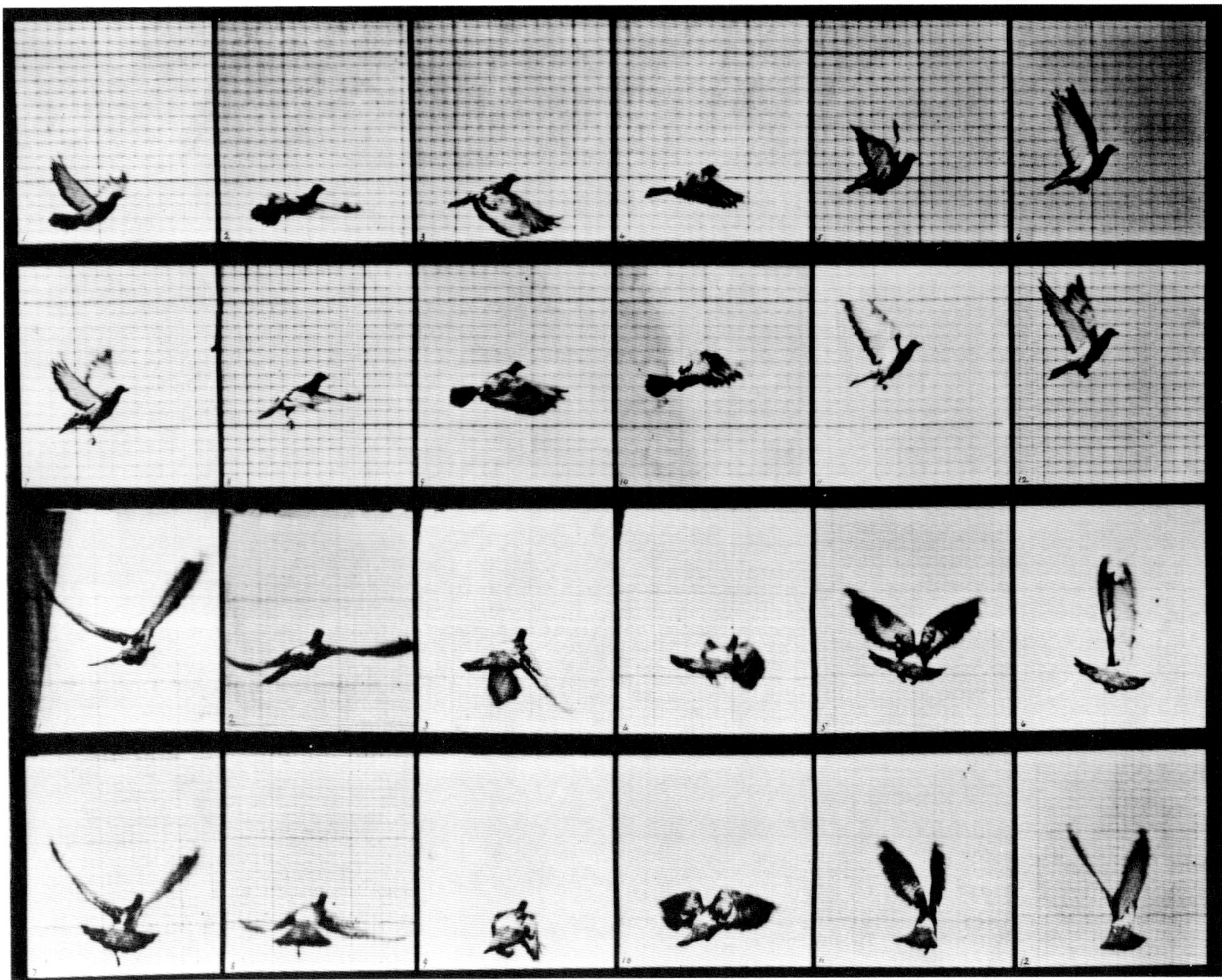

Fig. 18. Eadweard Muybridge, Eagle in Flight, *1887. Photo-engraving (pl. 757 in* Animal Locomotion). *Library of Congress, Washington, D.C.*

immediate specificity. Audubon further observed of the golden-eye: "Happy being! . . . endowed with a cunning . . . which preserves you from many at least of the attempts of man to destroy you."[28] This last involvement of man, in the presence of the hunter behind and ourselves in front of the birds of *Right and Left,* is the new and consummate drama.

[28] Davidson, *Audubon,* pl. 248.

Whatever the imagery of art or mind that gestated in the creation of this painting, Homer labored physically over its execution. If we now come back to the work itself for closer scrutiny, the eye can readily see that this is a thickly painted canvas, with occasional overlayers of pigment and reworkings of certain portions. The pasty and opaque quality of the paint textures contributes to our sense of an ultimately impenetrable space. We probably want to read the faintly glinting light on the sea under the left-hand duck's wing as a mark of expanding distance, yet this remains elusive, uncertain. Just the tiniest touch of red appears at the intersection of this light gray zone with the darker gray above, and a second is visible at the same level in the center of the picture. Are we to understand this as the

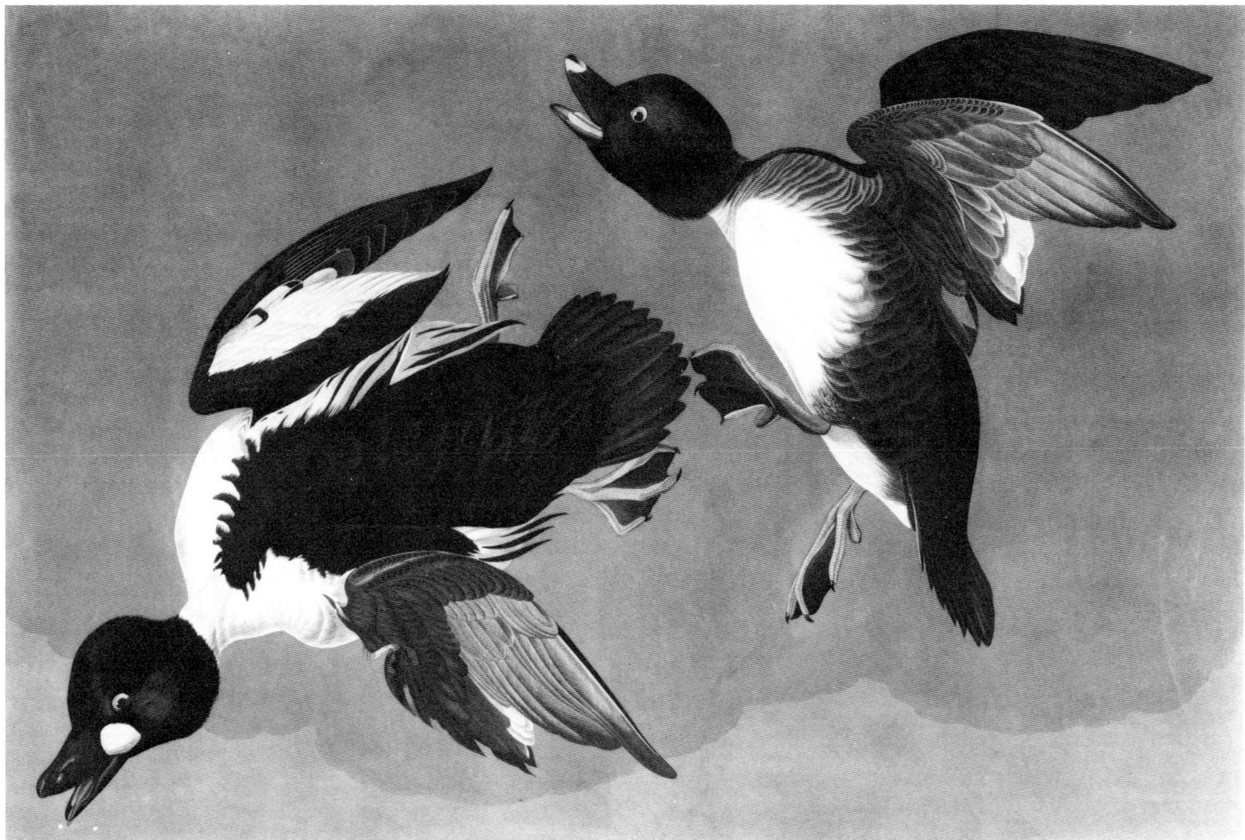

Fig. 19. John James Audubon, Golden-Eye Duck, *1827/1838. Color engraving by Robert Havell (Plate CCCXLII in* Birds of America). *National Gallery of Art, Washington, D.C.*

obscured rays of late wintry sunlight? Another gratuitous short stroke of red appears between the two ducks in the upper center, but this describes nothing identifiable. Hints of similar red pigment are apparent as an underlayer across much of the upper gray-white strip of cloud. These various suggestions of red are related to, yet different from, the more orange blast of the shotgun below and function as reminders of light as well as blood.

As Roger Stein has already observed, this is a notably monochromatic painting. Intentionally this restraint forces the viewer to probe the nuances of the existing color variations and to appreciate gradually the visual force which emerges to surprise us in this canvas. Between the upper passage of warm reddish-gray clouds and the lower green-white wave crests Homer fixes the more neutral tans of the two ducks. Almost twenty years before, La Farge had made critical remarks to Homer about using too much brown in his paintings. In response Homer executed *The West Wind* (1891; Addison Gallery, Andover, Massachusetts), with a virtually monochromatic palette of browns and beiges.[29] The resulting austerity was completely expressive of the bleakness of a lone woman battling the elements at the rise of a sand dune. In *Right and Left,* as in other late canvases, Homer again exploited a unifying palette of somber tonalities to complement the starkness of his subject matter.

29 Beam, *Homer,* 97.

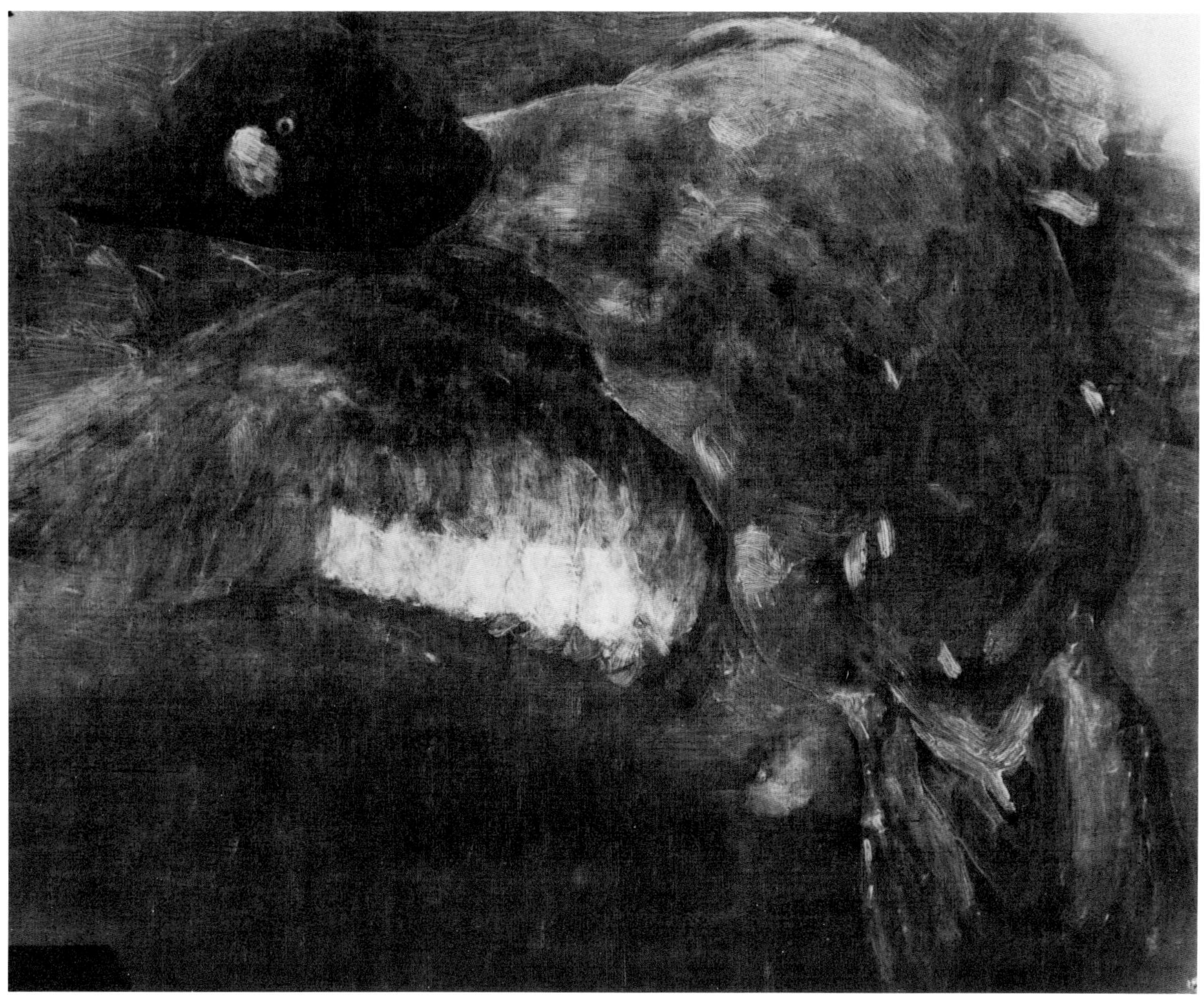

Fig. 20. X-ray of left portion of Right and Left. *Photo: National Gallery of Art, Washington, D.C.*

The heavy overpainting at the top edge of the oil is evident. It is also clear from an x-ray of the left-hand bird (fig. 20) that Homer modulated the contours of its outstretched wing to the left and its white breast above. In each area he has lowered the profile slightly and rounded it off. This brushwork serves to sharpen those two straining parts of its body, while also strengthening the rhythms of the repeating arc forms. Homer corrected or reworked on occasion both his watercolors and oils. In some instances he is known to have cut down a watercolor to new proportions, and in 1893 he repainted the entire left half of an oil he had begun in Tynemouth a decade earlier.[30] The adjustments we find in *Right and Left* (fig. 21) are not so radical but, rather, reflect the care and intensity of his creative energy in this work.

[30] See Wilmerding, *Homer*, 162-163, 189.

Although the title of the painting seems perfect for the image and one apparently satisfactory to Homer, it was not his invention. Downes tells us that the artist gave it no title when he sent it to Knoedler's gallery in New York for exhibition and sale. A visiting sportsman is said to have exclaimed "Right and left!" on seeing the

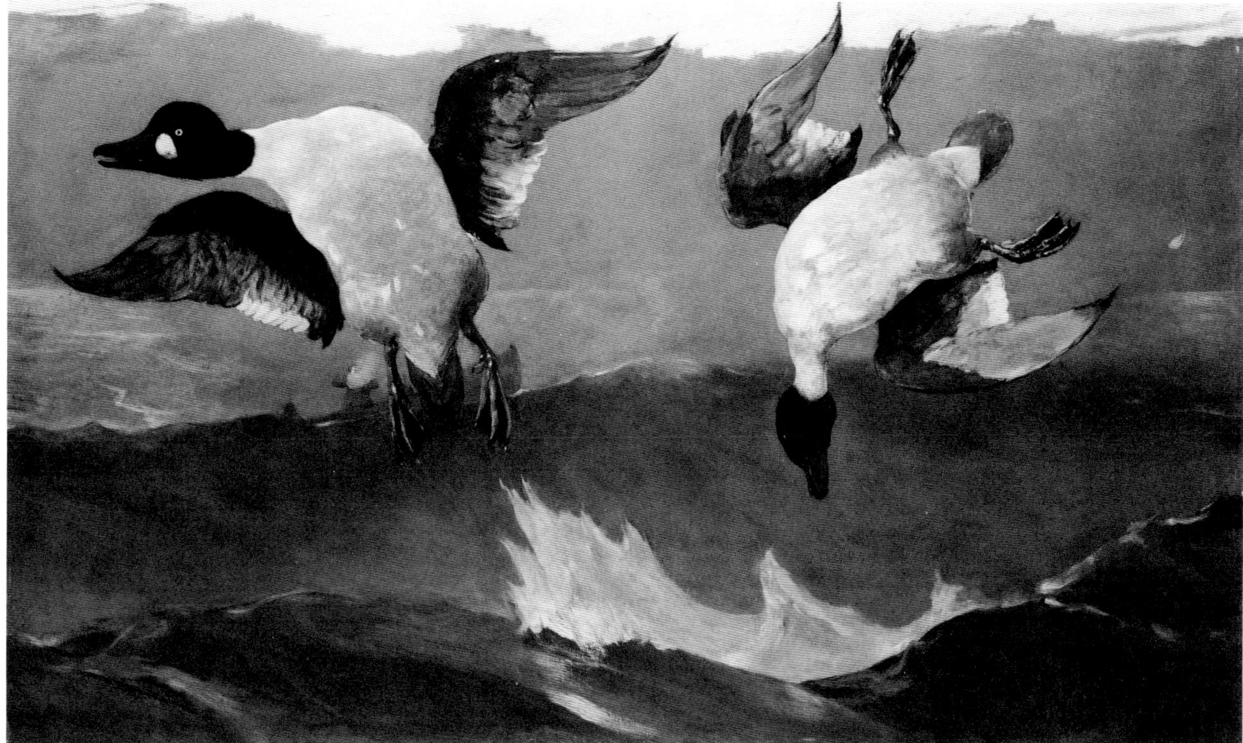

Fig. 21. Winslow Homer, Right and Left, *1909. Oil on canvas. National Gallery of Art, Washington, D.C.; Gift of the Avalon Foundation 1951*

painting, having in mind the hunter who brings down a bird with succeeding shots from his double-barreled shotgun.[31] Randall Morgan of Philadelphia bought the canvas and loaned it for the first time in 1910, under the title by which it has since been known, to an exhibition at the Pennsylvania Academy of the Fine Arts. The painting remained in the Morgan family until it was acquired for the National Gallery in 1951.

The sportsman's exclamation has been taken for granted ever since, though it has been by no means clear or agreed as to which duck has been shot first and just what moment of mortality we are witnessing. The remark of the Knoedler's visitor would suggest he assumed both birds had been shot dead. Samuel Green states that the duck on the left is "arising from a stormy sea, the other shot down and falling."[32] By contrast, Roger Stein reads death first in the rising duck from "the flash of the gun behind the limp webbed feet of the left hand bird."[33] Yet we do not know which blast, the first or the second from the shotgun, is depicted in the distance. If the second, then both birds have been hit. Yet the one on the left does seem strangely alert in its rising posture, in its indication of quick motion to our left, and in its bright yellow eye which fixes us as much as its sense of direction. If we are witness to the first shot, the left-hand bird may have limp feet; but these surely may be due as much to rapid upward flight as to death. Yet who is to say categorically that the duck to the right is the one shot, for his downward dart is utterly typical of the species diving from an unexpected threat. The fact is that Homer gives us these multiple ambiguities and leaves them

[31] Downes, *Homer,* 245.

[32] Green, *American Art,* 403.

[33] Roger Stein, "Structure as Meaning," 75.

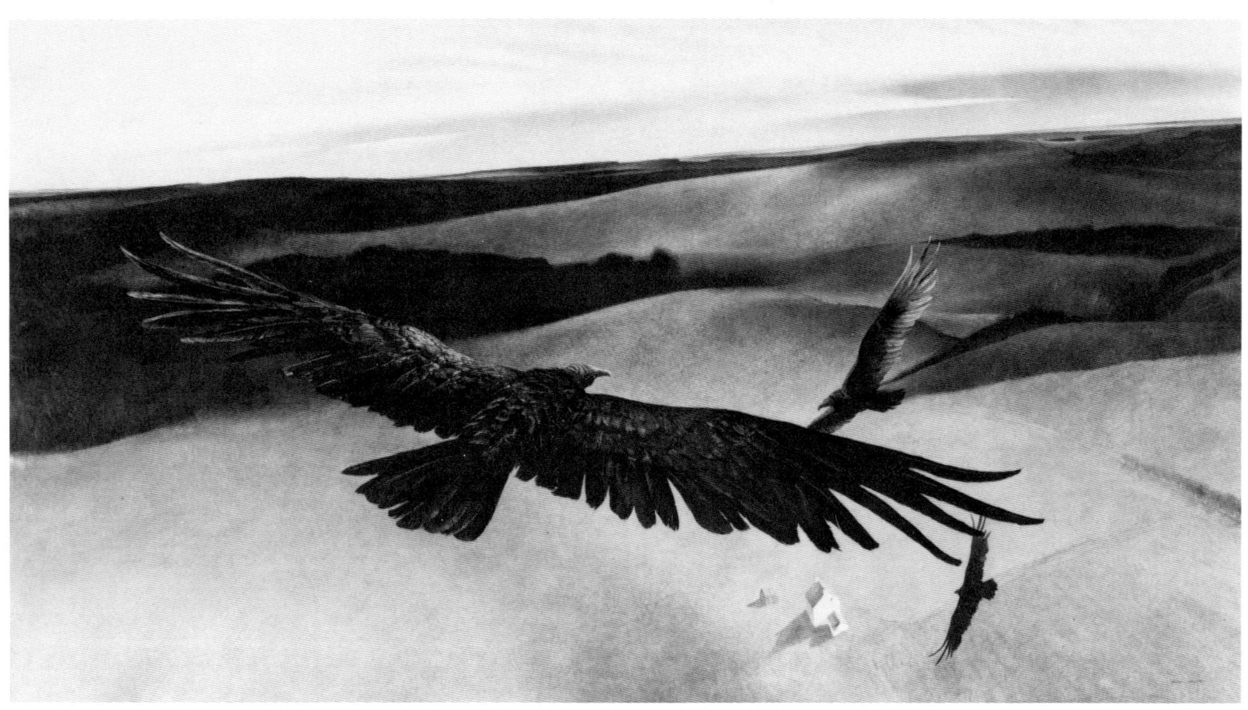

Fig. 22. Andrew Wyeth, Soaring, *1950. Tempera. Shelburne Museum, Inc., Shelburne, Vermont*

mysteriously unanswered. A more proper and profound reading would be that we observe that very moment when the shotgun blast explodes, but has not yet hit, or is—at the instant we arrive—hitting the first bird. In short, we are present at that mystical split-second juncture *between* life and death. In truth these ducks are as much alive as dead, in all the ironic meanings of the term "still life."

Homer was not a religious individual or artist, yet this painting addresses those ineffable issues of the relationship between body and spirit. Although the postures of his birds derive foremost from the ornithology of Audubon's observed world, there are inevitable psychological associations we make with a fall to death and a rising up to life. Like Pope's *Trumpeter Swan* (fig. 14), Homer's ducks spread out their wings in the pose of martyrs, recalling both a crucifixion and ascension. The mystery of life and death here leads us to meditate on not mere survival but immortality for these living creatures who momentarily stay air, water, and gravity.

Such a work of art has increased significance every time we come to it, and Homer's *Right and Left* is as strong as any painting ever produced in America. It has continued to summarize Homer's own contribution to the native realist tradition, while also effecting an influence on American painters of subsequent generations. We need only glance at Andrew Wyeth's sweeping tempera *Soaring*, 1950 (fig. 22), to realize its distant legacy. Wyeth, one of the leading interpreters of American realism in the twentieth century, has chosen to exploit the forceful evocation of similar dislocations in scale, an unexpected aerial vantage point, and figural abstractions belonging equally to art and nature. The lonely alienation viewers feel in

Wyeth's painting in part belongs to the modern spirit.[34] Commented Wyeth many years after painting *Soaring*: "I admire Winslow Homer's *Right and Left.* It's very American, very powerful, and a marvelous piece of very abstract design, taken from nature without getting sentimental. It's a very contemporary picture and, I think, his most outstanding."[35]

In its own modern way *Right and Left* embodies those intimations of chaos and disorientation Henry Adams described in his *Education* in 1907: a world on the threshold of disorder and relativity, moving away from sure, fixed absolutes of the past. Like Homer, Adams was fascinated with polarities and opposites (the Virgin and the dynamo, *Mont Saint-Michel and Chartres* and *The Education,* male and female, unity and multiplicity). In this view we can regard the painter's ducks fixed as if in some magnetic field of force, at a point of tension rather than rest. Yet Audubon lyrically saw the common golden-eye able to "arise on whistling wings, and swifter than Jer Falcon, speed away."[36] Homer, too, saw nature transcendent, in this work above all.

[34] See the discussion of this by Wanda M. Corn, *The Art of Andrew Wyeth,* exh. cat., Fine Arts Museums of San Francisco (1973), esp. 92-165.

[35] Quoted in *Art News* (Nov. 1977), 103.

[36] Marshall Davidson, *Audubon,* pl. 248.

For their editorial assistance I would like to thank Polly Roulhac and Don Mathison.

Biographical Sketches

JOHN OLIVER HAND has been curator of northern European painting at the National Gallery of Art since 1973. He received his M.A. degree from the University of Chicago and his M.F.A. and Ph.D. degrees from Princeton University. His doctoral dissertation dealt with the sixteenth-century Antwerp painter Joos van Cleve.

BETSY JEAN ROSASCO is currently finishing her doctoral thesis on the sculptures of the Château of Marly during the reign of Louis XIV and expects to receive her doctorate from the Institute of Fine Arts of New York University in June, 1980. She received her M.A. from the Institute of Fine Arts in 1971, and her B.A. from Smith College in 1968. She was a Chester Dale Fellow at the Metropolitan Museum of Art (1973-1975), a David E. Finley Fellow at the National Gallery of Art (1975-1978), and a Junior Fellow at the Center for Studies in Landscape Architecture at Dumbarton Oaks (1978-1979).

ANNE MARKHAM SCHULZ received her Ph.D. from the Institute of Fine Arts at New York University. She is the author of *The Sculpture of Bernardo Rossellino and His Workshop* (Princeton, 1977) and *Niccolò di Giovanni Fiorentino and Venetian Sculpture of the Early Renaissance,* CAA Monographs, xxxiii (New York, 1978), as well as numerous articles on Renaissance art. She has taught at Brown University.

PHILIP L. SOHM, assistant professor in the Department of Fine Art, University of Toronto, received his Ph.D. from The Johns Hopkins University; his dissertation on the Scuola di San Marco in Venice will be published in the Garland Series. He held a Kress

Fellowship at the National Gallery of Art (1976-1977). His publications include articles on the staircases of the *scuole grandi* in *Architectura* and on Palma Vecchio's *Sea Storm* in the Canadian journal RACAR.

JOHN WILMERDING is curator of American art and senior curator at the National Gallery of Art. Previously he taught at Dartmouth College, where he held the Leon E. Williams Professorship. He has also been a visiting professor at Harvard, Yale, and the University of Maryland. He is the author of a dozen books on American art, including monographs on Robert Salmon, Fitz Hugh Lane, and Winslow Homer. In 1973 he was awarded a Guggenheim Fellowship to write *American Art* in the Pelican History of Art series. His most recent publication is *American Light: The Luminist Movement,* completed in conjunction with an exhibition at the National Gallery in the spring of 1980.

Changes in Attribution

The following changes in attribution are the result of scholarly research based on the latest art historical investigations and scientific examinations. It is the policy of the National Gallery of Art to publish these changes regularly. The following changes in attribution were made during 1978-1979.

PAINTING

Number	*Former Attribution*	*Change to:*
1110	Albrecht Altdorfer *The Fall of Man* Samuel H. Kress Collection 1952	Workshop of Albrecht Altdorfer
1222	American School, 18th century *Girl in Pink Dress* Gift of Edgar William and Bernice Chrysler Garbisch 1953	Beardsley Limner
1274	American School, 18th century *Charles Adams Wheeler* Gift of Edgar William and Bernice Chrysler Garbisch 1953	Beardsley Limner
2320	American School, 19th century *Blacksmith Shop* Gift of Edgar William and Bernice Chrysler Garbisch 1966	Francis A. Beckett
694	Jan Vermeer *Young Girl with a Flute* Widener Collection 1942	Circle of Jan Vermeer

	Number	Former Attribution	Changed to:
		Follower of Jan Vermeer	
	54	*The Lacemaker*	Imitator of Jan Vermeer
	55	*The Smiling Girl*	
		Andrew W. Mellon Collection 1937	
SCULPTURE		Honoré Daumier	
	A-1638	*Man of Affairs*	Imitator of Honoré Daumier
		Rosenwald Collection 1953	
		Clodion	French School, 19th century
	A-1619	*Bacchant*	
	A-1620	*Bacchante*	
	A-1621	*Bacchante*	
		Samuel H. Kress Collection 1952	
		Robert Le Lorrain	Benoît Massou, Anselme Flamen, and Nicolas (?) Rebillé *A Garden Allegory: The Dew and Zephyr Cultivating Flowers*
	A-1630	*The Dew*	
		Samuel H. Kress Collection 1952	
		Studio of Andrea della Robbia	Andrea della Robbia
	A-11	*Madonna and Child with Cherubim*	
		Andrew W. Mellon Collection 1937	
GRAPHIC ARTS (drawings)	B-22,379	Giacomo Guardi *The Island of Malamocco* Samuel H. Kress Collection 1963	Francesco Guardi *The Fortress of San Andrea from the Lagoon*
	B-21,675	Francesco Guardi *Classic Ruins (with lake in background)* Howard Sturges Bequest 1955	Giacomo Guardi *Capriccio of Classical Ruins on a Shore*
	B-21,676	Francesco Guardi *Classic Ruins* Howard Sturges Bequest 1955	Giacomo Guardi *Cappriccio of Classical Ruins with a Fortress*
	B-10,963	Luca Cambiaso *Birth of Edward the Second (?), The Birth of St. John the Baptist (?)* Rosenwald Collection 1943	Giulio Benso *Birth Scene*
	B-1679	Jean-Honoré Fragonard Drawing for *The Widow of Ephesus (La Matrone d'Ephèse)* in *La Fontaine's Fables* (Contes) Widener Collection 1942	After Jean-Honoré Fragonard
	B-22,374	Jean-Honoré Fragonard *Interior of a Farmhouse with Figures* Samuel H. Kress Collection 1964	French, 18th century

Number	Former Attribution	Changed to:
B-22,375	Jean-Honoré Fragonard *Landscape at St. Tropez with Figures* Samuel H. Kress Collection 1964	French, second half of 18th century *L'Allée de Grenadiers*
B-22,378	Jean-Honoré Fragonard *View in the Villa d'Este* Samuel H. Kress Collection 1964	French, 18th century *Park of an Italian Villa*
B-24,231	Jean-Honoré Fragonard *Le Voile des Amours (The Veil of Cupids)* Gift of Mrs. Snowden A. Fahnestock 1965	French, 18th century
B-14,305	Thomas Gainsborough *Sketch of the Painter's Two Daughters* Gift of Myron A. Hofer 1947	Attributed to George Frost *Two Girls in a Landscape*
B-22,380	Mme. Adelaide Labille-Guiard *Portrait of a Lady* Samuel H. Kress Collection 1963	French, late 18th century
B-22,394	Hubert Robert *The Seesaw* Samuel H. Kress Collection 1964	Style of Hubert Robert
B-21,732	Gabriel de Saint-Aubin *Lady's Head* Howard Sturges Bequest 1956	Style of Gabriel de Saint-Aubin
B-25,280	Gabriel de Saint-Aubin *Portrait of the Artist with his Younger Brother, Augustin Saint-Aubin* Andrew Mellon Fund 1968	Imitator of Gabriel de Saint-Aubin
B-15,259	Joseph Mallord William Turner(?) *Landscape* (perhaps a study for the *Liber Studiorum)* Gift of R. Horace Gallatin 1949	English, 19th century
B-22,399	Claude-Joseph Vernet *Port Scene* Samuel H. Kress Collection 1964	Follower of Claude-Joseph Vernet